Collins

Easy Learning

GCSE Foundation

English

Revision Guide

FOR AQA A

About the revision guide

This revision guide covers the content for Paper 1 and Paper 2 for English GCSE AQA/A. It is designed to help you get the best grade in your GCSE Foundation written exams by showing you the reading and writing skills you need to succeed.

The book covers:
Paper 1 Section A
Paper 2 Section A
Papers 1 and 2 Section B

The sample student answers in the book have been given an approximate grade on the page and/or a comment for guidance, so you can easily see the level of the answer and compare it to your own.

Special features

Questions or **Tasks** at the end of each topic provide a quick way to practise the key points. You can find the answers to these on pages 88–94.

Top Tips pick out extra exam techniques to help you improve your grade.

Good points analyse and comment on examples of student answers to help you understand why they have been given the grade highlighted on the page.

How To Improve boxes show the main points to improve in the sample student answers in order to move up a grade.

Cross-references give the pages where you can find more information about a particular skill or technique.

Pages 8–9

Revision and practice

Use this book alongside *Easy Learning GCSE English Foundation & Higher Exam Practice Workbook for AQA A.* The workbook contains exam-style questions so you can practise what you've learnt in this revision guide. You can check your answers to the workbook online at: **www.collinseducation.com/easylearning**.

Published by Collins
An imprint of HarperCollins*Publishers*
77–85 Fulham Palace Road
Hammersmith
London W6 8JB

Browse the complete Collins catalogue at www.collinseducation.com

© HarperCollins*Publishers* Limited 2007

10 9 8 7 6 5 4 3 2 1

ISBN-13 978-0-00-726071-3

The authors assert their moral right to be identified as the authors of this work.

British Library Cataloguing in Publication Data
A Catalogue record for this publication is available from the British Library

Written by Kim Richardson and Keith Brindle
Consultant: Keith Brindle
Edited by Sue Chapple
Design by Linda Miles, Lodestone Publishing Limited
Illustrations by Chi Leung, Jennie Sergeant, Sarah Wimperis
Index compiled by Marie Lorimer
Printed and bound by

Acknowledgements
The Authors and Publishers are grateful to the following to reproduce copyright material:

Inside Soap Magazine, 3–9 February 2007. Reprinted with the kind permission of Inside Soap Magazine. Article courtesy of Yorkshire Evening Post, 15th May, 2003.

Reprinted with permission. Extract from 'Gaze and Laze', from Take A Break Magazine, 20th November, 2003. Reprinted with permission of Bauer UK. Extract from article entitled 'Q: Are we a nation of workaholics?', from Psychologies, January 2007. Reprinted with permission. Extract from ''Toxic' Rust-Bucket is Here', from The Sun, 13th November, 2003. Reprinted with permission. Screengrab of www.bbc.co.uk/holiday © BBC. Reprinted with permission of BBC. Extract from 'Grand Inquisitor' by Robin Day, published by Weindenfeld & Nicholson. Reprinted with permission. 'Nivea for Men' advert reprinted by kind permission of Beiersdorf UK. 'Vultures' by Chinua Achebe, from Beware Soul Brother published by Heinmann Educational. Reprinted with permission. 'Not My Business' by Niyi Osundare, from Songs of the Seasons published by Heinemann Educational Books, Nigeria, 1990. Reprinted with the kind permission of the author. 'Two Scavengers in a Truck, Two Beautiful People in a Mercedes' by Lawrence Ferlinghetti, from These Are My Rivers. Copyright © 1979 by Lawrence Ferlinghetti. Reprinted by permission of New Directions Publishing Corporation. From 'Limbo' by Kamau Braithwaite, from The Arrivants: A New World Trilogy published by OUP in 1973. Reprinted by permission of Oxford University Press. 'Love after Love' by Derek Walcott, from Collected Poems, published by Faber and Faber. Reprinted with permission of Faber and Faber Limited. 'This Room' by Imtiaz Dharker, from I Speak for the Devil published by Bloodaxe Books 2001. Reprinted by permission of the publisher, Bloodaxe Books. 'Presents from my Aunts in Pakistan' by Moniza Alvi, from The Country at My Heart, originally published by Oxford Paperbacks, 1993. Reprinted by permission of the current publisher, Bloodaxe Books. Extract from 'A Farewell to Arms' by Ernest Hemingway, published by Jonathan Cape. Used by permission of The Random House Group Limited. Extract from 'The Fight' by Norman Mailer, published by Penguin Books Limited. Reprinted with permission.

Photographs
The Authors and Publishers are grateful to the following for permission to reproduce photographs:

p. 11 Patrick Seegar/epa/Corbis
p. 13 Tim Mosenfelder/Corbis
p. 18 bdi-images.com (top); Photodisc/Getty (bottom)
p. 44 Rex Features

Whilst every effort has been made to trace the copyright holders, in cases where this has been unsuccessful, or if any have inadvertently been overlooked, the Publishers will be pleased to make the necessary arrangements at the first opportunity.

Contents

About your AQA/A English exam — 4

Reading media and non-fiction — 6

Fact and opinion	8
Following an argument	10
Language	14
Layout and presentational devices	18
How to refer to the text successfully	20
Analysing text types	21
Comparing texts	24
Raising your grade	26

Reading poems from different cultures and traditions — 28

Different cultures and traditions	30
Content, message and attitude	32
Structure	36
Language	38
Comparing two poems	42
Raising your grade	46

Writing skills — 48

Ideas and planning	50
Structure and paragraphs	52
Sentences	54
Vocabulary	56
Punctuation	58
Spelling and accuracy	60

Types of writing — 62

Writing to argue	62
Writing to persuade	66
Writing to advise	70
Writing to inform	74
Writing to explain	78
Writing to describe	82
Raising your grade	86

Answers — 88

Index — 95

About your AQA/A English exam

Exam papers

- There are two exam papers, Paper 1 and Paper 2.
- Each paper tests some reading skills and some writing skills.
- Each paper is worth 30% of the total marks you can get in your English GCSE.

See the chart opposite: **GCSE English at a glance**.

> *For more on these exam papers, see:*
> *pages 6–7 (Paper 1, Section A)*
> *pages 28–29 (Paper 2, Section A)*
> *pages 48–49 (Papers 1 and 2, Section B)*

The skills you are assessed on

- When the examiners mark your answers, they are looking for certain skills. These are called **assessment objectives**. This book covers all the assessment objectives for Reading and Writing.
- Speaking and listening skills are tested in your coursework, along with reading and writing skills.

The reading skills you are assessed on

In the Reading sections of each paper, you need to show that you:

- **understand what the texts are about**.
  This means explaining their content and purpose. You will need to refer to the texts in your answer.

- **can tell the difference between a fact and an opinion**.
  This means identifying facts and opinions in the text, and explaining how and why they have been used.

- **can write about how information is presented**.
  This means saying how effective you think the texts are at doing their job.

- **can follow an argument**.
  This means explaining what a writer is saying, and how they have put their ideas together.

- **understand the techniques that writers use**.
  This means commenting on the language they use, how they organise their texts and the way they present them on the page.

- **can compare texts**.
  This means explaining how one text is similar to, or different from, another. You need to refer to examples across both texts.

These skills are covered in the first two sections of this book: *Reading Media and Non-Fiction* (pages 6–27) and *Poetry from Different Cultures and Traditions* (pages 28–47).

The writing skills you are assessed on

In the Writing sections of each paper, you need to show that you:

- **can communicate clearly and imaginatively**.
  This means writing so that the reader understands what you are saying and is interested in it.

- **have a clear idea of purpose and audience**.
  This means being able to write in a particular form (e.g. a letter or a newspaper article) and for a particular audience (e.g. young people).

- **can organise your writing**.
  This means using sentences and paragraphs, and giving your writing some sort of structure.
- **can use a range of words and sentence structures**.
  This means using a varied vocabulary, techniques such as repetition and contrast, and different types of sentence for different effects.
- **can punctuate and spell correctly**.
  This means using a range of punctuation, such as full stops, commas and questions marks, and showing that you can spell accurately.

These skills are covered in the final two sections of this book: *Writing Skills* (pages 48–61) and *Types of Writing* (pages 62–87).

GCSE English at a glance

GCSE English Specification A

This tests your reading skills. You will be asked about two or three non-fiction and media texts that you haven't seen before. (pages 6–27)

Paper 1	30% of the total marks
1¾ hours	

| Section A | Reading non-fiction and media | 15% |
| Section B | Writing: argue, persuade, advise | 15% |

This tests your writing skills. You will be asked to write to argue, persuade or advise. (pages 62–73)

Paper 2	30% of the total marks
1½ hours	

This tests your reading skills. You will be asked about the poems from different cultures in your Anthology. (pages 28–47)

| Section A | Reading poetry from different cultures and traditions | 15% |
| Section B | Writing: inform, explain, describe | 15% |

This tests your writing skills. You will be asked to write to inform, explain or describe. (pages 74–85)

Coursework	40% of the total marks

| Speaking and listening | | |
| 3 assessed activities | | 20% |

These are the pieces of coursework that your teacher has asked you to do. They are not covered in this revision guide.

| Reading: | Shakespeare | 5% |
| | Prose study | 5% |

| Writing: | Media | 5% |
| | Original writing | 5% |

Paper 1 Section A: Reading media and non-fiction

Key points

- Paper 1 Section A will focus on **two or three different texts**. You will not have seen these texts before. They will be **media** and **non-fiction** texts.

- In an hour, you will have to answer about **four to six questions**.

- This section of the exam counts for **15% of your total mark**.

The texts

- At least one text will be a **media text**. This means a piece of writing from a newspaper, magazine or website, or a printed leaflet, brochure or advice sheet.

- There will probably also be a **non-fiction text** which might not be from the media. This could be an extract from a biography, an autobiography or an information text such as an encyclopedia.

The exam paper

Paper 1 Section A: Foundation Tier

In addition to this paper you will require:
- Text 1: *Need a break? Want a change? Why not try Bognor ...?*, from a weekend magazine
- Text 2: *Ancient art of relaxing*, from the *Sunday Express*

READING: NON-FICTION AND MEDIA TEXTS

Answer all the questions in Section A.
Spend approximately 60 minutes on Section A.

1 Re-read Text 1: *Need a break? Want a change? Why not try Bognor ....?*

   a) Why does the writer think it is good to take holidays in Britain? Answer using your own words. *(6 marks)*

   b) Which do you think are the writer's best two points, and why? *(2 marks)*

   c) How does the writer try to make us agree with him? Write about:
   - the use of fact and opinion
   - any other techniques he uses to make us agree with him. *(6 marks)*

2 Next, re-read Text 2: *Ancient art of relaxing*.

   a) Who do you think this text has been written for? Explain your opinion. *(4 marks)*

Finally, look at both texts together.

   b) How do the texts try to interest the reader? Write about:
   - each writer's use of language
   - presentational devices in *Ancient art of relaxing*. *(9 marks)*

   Total: 27 marks

You will be given these texts in full in the exam. They are both media texts. (They are not provided here.)

Remember to spend up to 10 minutes of this time reading the texts carefully, as well as the questions themselves.

Note that this question only relates to Text 1. Don't write about both texts here!

This question only relates to Text 2.

The final question usually asks you to compare the texts. This means commenting on things that are similar and things that are different.

The marks are given for each question. Use this information to help you time yourself – don't spend a lot of time on this question!

The skills you will be assessed on

The questions that you are asked in Paper 1 Section A will test certain reading skills. This page outlines the skills that are tested (on the left), and explains what you have to do to get good marks (on the right).

The skill you need to show	How to get good marks

1 Understanding what the texts are about

Pages 8–27

- Find **information** in the texts.
- Explain **what the texts are about**.
- Recognise their **form**, e.g. a magazine article.
- Understand their **purpose**, e.g. to persuade the reader.
- Recognise their **target audience** (who they are written for).
- **Refer to the texts** in your answer, to provide evidence for your views.

2 Understanding about facts and opinions

Pages 8–9

- Identify **facts and opinions** in the texts.
- Explain **how** they have been used by the writer, and **why**.
- Explain their **purpose** in the text and their **effect** on the reader.
- Give an opinion on **how successfully** you think the texts do their job.

3 Following an argument

Pages 10–13

- Understand what a writer says – their **point of view**.
- Explain the **key points** they are using.
- Identify the **evidence** used to support the key points.
- Identify the **techniques** used by the writer to persuade the reader.
- Point out what you think makes the argument **convincing** (or not).

4 Understanding the techniques that writers use

Pages 14–21

- Identify where the writers have used **language to create an effect**, e.g. powerful words, exaggeration, repetition or contrast.
- Explain **how** these techniques are **effective**, and **how** they suit the **purpose** or **audience**.
- Describe the **structure** of the text and any **presentational devices**, e.g. headlines, pictures, bullet points, and say why they have been used.

5 Choosing the right information and comparing texts

Pages 22–27

- **Select the right information** from the texts to answer the question, e.g. by skimming or scanning.
- Write about the ways in which the texts are **similar** or **different**.
- **Refer to examples** across both texts.

Fact and opinion

Key points

- You need to **identify facts and opinions** in one or more texts.
- You need to write about **how they are used**.
- You may need to **compare** the use of fact and opinion in two different texts.

Identifying facts and opinions

- A **fact** is something that can be proved to be true, e.g. *Most people do not smoke.* Usually, there is evidence to back it up.
- An **opinion** is someone's belief, e.g. *Non-smokers have a happier life.* This is someone's point of view – your own view may be different.
- Many texts are a **mixture** of fact and opinion.

The article below is from the magazine *Inside Soap*. The facts are in blue. The opinions are in orange.

'Flamboyant' and 'mouthy' only in the judgement of the writer.

The spokesperson did make this statement.

This is just the spokesperson's own view.

Emmerdale fans had better brace themselves – as another member of the flamboyant Lambert family is about to descend on the village.

Actress Victoria Hawkins – who has previously starred in children's TV show Byker Grove – has been cast as mouthy Sharon Lambert, the estranged daughter of Woolpack landlady Val.

"We're delighted to welcome Victoria to the Emmerdale cast," said a spokesperson for the soap. "Sharon's going to cause a lot of trouble for Val. The pair have a very rocky relationship."

Some people could disagree.

It is true that Victoria Hawkins has been in Byker Grove and is going to join the cast of Emmerdale.

Writing about how facts and opinions are used

- Refer to the main **purpose** of the piece. For example, it may be mainly to provide information, in which case facts would be used more than opinions.
- Refer to the **audience** of the piece. For example, it may be people who could buy a product, in which case powerful opinions would be used to persuade them.
- Give **examples** from the text to support your ideas.

The writer's purpose is to give viewers some news about soaps, but also to persuade them to watch the programme. So there is a mixture of fact and opinion. The facts about how Sharon Lambert is related to the landlady Val are surrounded by opinions about the characters ('flamboyant', 'mouthy'), what is going to happen ('going to cause a lot of trouble') and the effect on the fans (they 'had better brace themselves') ...

Good Points

- The student explains why fact and opinion are both used, by referring to the writer's purpose.
- Suitable examples are used (or referred to) to support the ideas.
- This is likely to develop into a Grade C answer.

The next extract is from the *Yorkshire Evening Post*.

- In this extract, there are more facts than opinions.

- The purpose of the article is to report a story, not to sell something.

- The writer includes opinions from Graham.

- Graham uses facts to make the opinions believable, and to encourage people to support them.

 Top Tip!

Remember that facts can be used in different ways. Some facts simply present information. Others back up a writer's opinions, so their purpose is more persuasive.

A couple celebrating their 40th birthdays have asked for donations to charity instead of presents.

Graham and Chris Lingard of Ilkley both support Christian Aid, the churches' charity which raises money to help struggling Third World countries.

Their birthdays are close to each other and they decided on a joint party as part of this week's nationwide Christian Aid collection week.

Graham said: 'We both wanted to highlight how unfair our world is, and support a charity that works to help change this injustice.

'The problems facing Africa — **opinion** are hard for us even to imagine. Currently – due to chronic poverty, coupled with recurring drought – 38 million people simply do not have enough to eat. In 2005 AIDS alone killed — **fact** over 2 million people in sub-Saharan Africa,' he said.

Comparing texts

If the use of facts and opinions has to be compared in two texts, follow this plan:

- Paragraph 1: Write about the **first text** and how facts and opinions are used.

- Paragraph 2: Write about the **second text** and how facts and opinions are used.

- Paragraph 3: **Compare the two texts** and discuss whether their use of fact/opinion is the same or different.

This student is comparing how fact and opinion are used in the articles from *Inside Soap* and the *Yorkshire Evening Post*. This is how she starts the three paragraphs:

> (Paragraph 1) The first text relies heavily on opinions, for example ... This is because the purpose of the text ...
>
> (Paragraph 2) The second text, by contrast, begins with facts ... This is because ...
>
> (Paragraph 3) In conclusion, the texts are very different, but each suits its purpose ...

Task

Use the sentence starters above to complete this task:
Compare how fact and opinion are used in the articles from *Inside Soap* and the *Yorkshire Evening Post*.

Following an argument

Key points

- An **argument** is a structured way of putting forward an opinion about something.

- You need to show that you can **follow an argument**.

- This means identifying the writer's **point of view**.

- It will also mean showing **how the argument has been put together**. This means commenting on its **structure**, **language** and any **techniques** used.

Top Tip!

Don't simply repeat the content of the argument. You will need to put the argument into your own words, and comment on how it is structured and how language is used.

The writer's point of view

- The writer's **point of view** is their **attitude** to the subject of the text. For example, the point of view of the writer of the article below is that people are obsessed by watching sport.

- Identifying the point of view will help you explain the text's **purpose**, or why it was written. The writer's purpose in the article below is to show how bad the situation is, and to say what to do about it.

Structure

- When commenting on the structure of an argument, try to identify:

  – the **introduction**. This sets out the subject of the argument and shows the writer's viewpoint.

  – the **key points**. The argument is developed with some key points, usually backed by **evidence**. Often there is one key point in each paragraph.

  – the **conclusion**. This sums up the writer's point of view. It is a final statement to persuade the reader.

- Also try to spot where the writer attacks the **opposite viewpoint**. They do this to make their own argument stronger.

Look at the article about sport below and on page 11. (Only the first and last paragraphs have been given in full.) The notes show how the writer has structured the argument.

Paragraph 1: the writer's main point – that we are obsessed by sport.

What is it that makes people believe that watching sport is the most important activity known to man? Let's face it, we only live for seventy years – eighty if we're lucky – and yet so many people waste so much time watching pretty brainless bodies chasing a ball round a patch of grass; and often spend hundreds of pounds for the privilege. Failing that, they are glued to the game on TV. And when they are dead, what then? A life has been wasted, potential squandered, and nothing has been achieved.

Football fans, of course, see it differently …

This line of argument, however, is nothing short of ludicrous …

How many goals do we remember? How many service aces justify the time we spend watching …?

There must, surely, be more we could be doing …

Paragraph 2: the opposing viewpoint – that it's great to watch sport.

Paragraph 3: the opposing viewpoint is attacked.

Paragraphs 4 and 5: these add some key points to develop the argument.

Paragraph 6: the conclusion – that we need to change this situation to make society better.

So, what is the solution? In Britain we need to change the consciousness of the nation. Firstly, people need educating to realise that we could do more useful things to develop ourselves and – just imagine! – help others. Secondly, we need to remove the cult of the sport star and, instead, lay much more emphasis on those who do something worthwhile. How much better it would be, for example, if children grew up wanting to be a doctor, rather than Wayne Rooney.

Writing about structure

How could you summarise the way the argument in the article about sport has been put together? You could begin like this:

The article begins by pointing out that we waste our time watching sport. The writer makes his point of view very clear at the start, by making sportsmen seem unintelligent (we watch 'pretty brainless bodies chasing a ball'). We could do more with our lives: 'nothing has been achieved'.

The writer does go on to say that the fans have a different view. But immediately he attacks this view by suggesting it is 'ludicrous' or crazy. This helps to build up his own argument.

The middle section of the article adds further points to support the writer's argument. These are . . .

The article ends with a powerful conclusion. The writer suggests ways we could change things and improve the quality of our lives. The final sentence makes a strong contrast between being a doctor and being a footballer.

Grade C

Good Points

- This answer shows clear understanding of the structure: the beginning, the development of the argument, and the conclusion.
- It is organised logically – commenting on each section in turn.
- It quotes evidence from the text to back up the points made.

READING MEDIA AND NON-FICTION

Language

- Note how the language in an argument suits the **audience**:
    - *Hey, guys, don't diss me* is aimed at a young, cool audience.
    - *Those on the margins of society should not be condemned* is aimed at an intelligent, old-fashioned audience.
- Note how the language suits the **purpose** of the text:
    - If the argument is a proposal by a supermarket to build a large out-of-town store, the language will be calm, formal and logical.
    - If the writer is aiming to amuse the audience as much as persuade them, the language might be more exaggerated.

> **Top Tip!**
> When commenting on language in an argument, always refer to the purpose and audience of the writer.

Pages 14–17 (more on language use)

Techniques

- Identify the **techniques** that writers use to convince the reader.
- Some of these techniques for building an argument are described below.

    - **rhetorical questions**: questions asked for effect, that do not expect a reply, e.g.

    Don't we know this is lunacy? Is there nothing we can do?

    - **exaggeration**: overstating the case, to make the point even more strongly, e.g.

    There must be millions of rats just praying this law is passed and the sewers remain uncleaned …

    - **examples, repetition and lists**: details selected or emphasised to support a point, e.g.

    example:
    For example, half my children's presents lie unused after Christmas.
    repetition:
    Young people agree. Middle-aged people agree. Even older people agree.
    list:
    There are so many problems: homelessness, drug-taking, violence …

    - **personal stories or anecdotes**: brief stories used to show what happens, or what happened, e.g.

    Only last week, I was approached by a homeless person on my own street. She was not begging, however. She explained to me that …

    - **quotations**, usually from people with particular knowledge of the subject, e.g.

    "In my role as mayor, I see what happens and know what is wrong …"

    - **contrast**: setting contrasting points or images beside each other for effect, e.g.

    On one side there are the rich, arguing for lower taxes. On the other side sit the poor, who know that more money has to be raised to protect the health service.

    - **humour**, such as sarcasm: used to get the reader on the writer's side, e.g.

    This is the greatest victory since Waterton Road Under 7s trounced Snapethorpe in the Lupset Women's Group's Minor Footie League in 1959.

> **Top Tip!**
> When you identify the techniques a writer has used to build an argument, use a quotation to make the technique clear for the examiner. Even better, explain how the technique helps the writer make their point.

You can see some of these techniques being used in this magazine article. A middle-aged man writes about what it is like to grow older.

They say that age is a state of mind. I think age happens when you can no longer watch pop music on TV without cringing. I was brought up on *Top of the Pops* – in fact I lived for my Thursday evening fix of the latest sounds. I was devastated when the show was axed. What do kids watch now? I decided to find out by sitting with my own children one evening.

Shock and dismay. The channel was called 'Kiss' – that should have been a warning in itself. And instead of some friendly, reliable old DJ fronting the show, there was a continuous stream of what appeared to be semi-naked girls faintly disguised as pop artists.

'How old is she?' I asked my son, aghast, as I watched one of them, who looked as if she should be in school.

'Chill, dad.'

'She just giggles and screams. And she's wearing underwear.'

'So? Don't we all?'

Then, the performances.

'Why do they do that?'

'What?'

'The rappers … Their hands … Why do they do that with their hands? No drier in the toilets?'

'It's what they do.'

'But why?'

It's weird when a whole part of your life has passed you by, but, frankly, you don't care because you are happier with your memories of Tony Blackburn and the Beatles and the Eurovision Song Contest and singers who had hair and sang and didn't have bodies with rings all over, like chain mail.

Of course, it's next stop afternoon bingo. Then a stair lift. And, frighteningly, what comes after that …?

Maybe I'll breathe deeply and try to appreciate the girls and the rappers. While I still can.

contrast of the 'old DJ' and the 'semi-naked girls'

personal story to help explain his point of view

humour to win the reader over

listing lots of **examples** can be powerful

exaggerated picture – overstating the case for effect

rhetorical question – he knows the answer (death)

humour – note also the short phrase to end

Question

What does the writer of this magazine article have to say about growing older, and how does he build his argument?

Briefly explain:

- the writer's point of view
- the structure of the argument
- how he uses language and techniques to win the reader over to his point of view.

Language

Key points

- You will be asked to write about the **language** used in one or two of the texts.
- This means picking out the most **obvious features**, such as:
  - sentences and paragraphs
  - vocabulary (the words used)
  - punctuation
  - imagery
  - the style of the language.

Top Tip!

When commenting on the language of a text, don't try to write about the whole text. Focus on two or three key points, and go into detail on each one.

Sentences and paragraphs

- Notice the **length of sentences**, and the way they are **constructed**. This can produce different effects, such as:
  - **Short sentences** sometimes suggest speed or excitement, e.g.

  He ran forward. The ball fell at his feet. He shot.

  - **Long sentences** can help describe an event, building to a climax, e.g.

  The crowds gasped as the top of the mountain blew away, clouds of ash shot hundreds of feet into the sky and rivers of lava, terrifying in the early dawn, shot upwards, then cascaded down into the valley.

- **Paragraphs**, too, can create different effects:

  – **Very short paragraphs** can be used to pick out the main details, or to speed the reader on. Popular newspaper articles often have short paragraphs so that they can be read more easily.

  – **Longer paragraphs** can provide more detail and analysis. Articles in more serious newspapers often have longer paragraphs.

Top Tip!

Look out for paragraphs of very different lengths. A one-sentence paragraph after a long paragraph, for example, aims to grab the reader's attention.

Vocabulary

- The sort of words used in a text can tell you a lot about the **purpose** of the text:

  – Powerful **adjectives**, such as 'fantastic' and 'appalling', are often used to **persuade** the reader.

  – **Commands**, such as 'follow' and 'begin', suggest that the writing is giving **instructions** or **advice**.

  – Words like 'since' and 'because' suggest that the writing is **explaining** something.

  – Words like 'however', 'nevertheless' and 'indeed' may come from writing that is **arguing** a case.

- The words used can also tell you about the **audience** for a text:

  – **Longer words** suggest a text is aimed at an intelligent readership.

  – A text containing **modern vocabulary**, for instance dealing with ICT and communications, could be targeting younger people or those in the industry.

  – A text containing **slang** might be aimed at teenagers.

  – Vocabulary associated with a **specific subject** would be used in a text aimed at specialists. For example, a geography textbook will contain lots of geographical terms.

Top Tip!

Notice any word that seems powerful or unusual. There will be a reason why the writer has used it, and it will be worth commenting on. For example, *The dog howled incessantly* is more powerful than *The dog barked and barked*. The effect is to emphasise the unhappy sound the dog made.

Punctuation

- Look out for exclamation marks and question marks. They have a purpose, e.g.

HOLLY HITS OUT!!

The double exclamation mark attracts attention and suggests excitement.

WHY AREN'T WE BEING TOLD THE TRUTH?

The question also attracts attention by addressing the reader directly.

Imagery

- **Imagery** means using words to paint a picture. If a writer describes her son's room as a 'dustbin', she is using the image of a dustbin to make you realise how messy the room is.

- **Similes** and **metaphors** are examples of imagery.

This short extract has three examples of imagery:

similes – the 'like' shows something is being compared to something else (an image)

They held us in a small room. We felt like condemned men and smelt like battery hens. We had no idea of the day or the time and dreaded the dull echoes of sharp boots and the crank of the lock on the door. It was an eternity of torture ...

metaphor – being imprisoned is described as a 'torture'

Top Tip!

When you comment on language, use the correct technical term if you can (e.g. simile), but the main thing is to describe what effect it has, and why the writer has used it.

Look at how this student has commented on the use of language in the extract above:

The writer uses imagery to show what their life was like. The simile 'like condemned men' stresses their desperate situation. Another simile ('smelt like battery hens') shows the terrible conditions they were kept in. They were like animals.

Finally, the metaphor 'eternity of torture' is used to express how long and painful it must have seemed to them at the time.

Grade C

Good Points

- Precise examples are given, backed up by quotations from the text.
- The effects of the language are discussed, not just identified (e.g. 'the simile ... stresses their desperate situation').
- Some technical terms are used, e.g. simile, metaphor.

Style

- A text may be **formal** – with a more serious tone, e.g. serious newspaper articles, job applications. Here are some common features of a formal text:
  - close attention to all the rules of English
  - more difficult words
  - longer sentences.

- A text may be **informal** – with a warmer or chattier tone, e.g. emails, advertisements and light magazine articles. Common features include:
  - less attention to the rules of grammar and punctuation
  - the use of slang
  - simpler and more direct words and sentences.

Top Tip!

Always give examples to back up your comments, e.g.

The first text is formal, using sentences like 'The government has taken a stance which ...', while the second text is less formal and targets drug users: 'Get real ...'

Stylistic techniques

- Writers use different stylistic techniques to create effects:
  - **addressing the reader** directly (especially with **rhetorical questions**), to add impact:

  Can this be acceptable?

  - **emotive language**, which touches the reader's feelings:

  They are tiny and cold and they are starving.

  - **exaggeration**:

  The royal family eats nothing but caviar for breakfast.

  - **contrasts**:

  The seabirds sing, while the fishermen starve.

  - **colloquial language**, as if people are chatting:

  If you want to pull, you have to impress the lads.

  - **suggestion**, where things are suggested rather than clearly stated:

  He met the girl of his dreams. He didn't come home that night.

  - **examples** and **quotations**, to give credibility to what is written:

  Only yesterday, a shop assistant said to me ...

  - **humour**, to get the audience on the side of the writer:

  There was more life in my popcorn than in this film.

  - **lists**, for emphasis:

  She packed the potatoes on top of the bananas, the bananas on top of the tomatoes and the tomatoes on top of the eggs.

Top Tip!

Identifying features like these and commenting on their effect gets you extra marks in the exam. Practise finding them in the magazines you read. Work out what effect the writer is trying to create.

This extract from a newspaper article uses several of the techniques above.

> So, the Prime Minister claims that he has an excellent track record, does he? An excellent track record of what – destroying all areas of British life?
>
> People are paying taxes they can't afford, waiting in traffic that never moves, facing ever-mounting debt and an impoverished old age ...

You could comment on the style like this:

The writer begins by addressing us directly, which gets our attention. When she says 'claims', it makes us think it's not true. The next sentence is another rhetorical question, which contrasts the 'excellent' track record with the actual destruction of British life. Exaggeration is used here ('all areas') for added effect.

The list of three examples helps to build up the evidence against the Prime Minister. Exaggeration is used again ('never moves') and some emotive language when the writer refers to poor old people. This aims to get us on her side.

Grade C

Good Points

- The effect of the language is described.
- The purpose of the writer is referred to.
- Quotations are used to prove the points being made.
- Some technical terms are used, e.g. rhetorical, emotive.

Question

This extract comes from *Take a Break* magazine. Its aim is to attract people to visit Capri.
Some of the features of the writer's language have been highlighted in red.
Match them up with the list of features in the box.

Gaze and laze

Take a break where the sun always shines

All eyes turn to the sea on this 30-mile stretch of Italy's western shore, considered one of the most beautiful coastlines in the world, where Campania gazes out into the Tyrrhenian reaches of the Mediterranean.

It takes in Sorrento, Positano, Salerno and Amalfi – which gives it the local name *Costiera Amalfitana* – and even extends into the sea.

Sitting off the coast like a satellite at the end of the peninsula, the island of Capri is just a 20-minute cruise away from Sorrento. Fram the port of Marina Grande it's a short ride by funicular railway to the labyrinth of narrow alleyways that make up Capri town.

But it is at Anacapri, the island's second town, that you'll find Capri's very own Garden of Eden, where mythological statues sit like sentinels surveying the deep blue waters. Or where classically draped figures from Italy's past appear to hold command over clouds fleeing across the contrasting blue of the sky.

Find an example of:

- exaggeration
- a simile
- direct address to reader
- a list
- a metaphor
- another simile

Layout and presentational devices

Key points

- You need to understand how **layout** and **presentational devices** are used in media texts.

- Layout means the way the page is arranged. Presentational devices are the different features that are used to create the layout, such as pictures and headlines.

- You will be expected to write about **why** these particular devices have been used.

Identifying the features

- Some common features used in media texts include:

strapline – a second-level headline which gives more details

introductory paragraph could be in bold print or with the first word capitalised

subheading – minor heading used to give a summary, or break up the text, or grab the reader's attention

heading – note the size and style. The main heading is called a headline. Here, block capitals are used for emphasis.

photograph – illustrations are often an important part of the design. How do they relate to the text?

caption – the text under a photograph or diagram which helps us understand it

columns – text often in columns to make it easier to read

PEACE AT LAST?

PM set to sign treaty at end of historic talks

ONLY LAST YEAR, the prospect of a resolution to the conflict seemed remote. Now, with all parties in agreement, there is a chance of peace.

Last chance

The Prime Minister faced tough questions yesterday

logo – an image that represents a product or company

font – the style of the typeface. The style, size and colour can vary throughout a text.

bold, italics, underlining – different ways of making words stand out

quotation – taken from a reviewer of the club and set apart, to make it stand out

slogan – a word or phrase linked with a product, so you can remember it

photographs and graphics – different kinds of illustration used for different purposes, e.g. the map to help people find the club

NITE STAR

The brightest club in town

8:30pm till 1:00am
Monday – Saturday

Tickets £10

NITE STAR
How to find us

"Nite Star? It's heaven!"

Top Tip!

Don't worry if you don't remember the correct terms for these features. You will gain credit if you do, but you get more marks for describing them and saying what is important about them.

Writing about presentational devices

- Don't just describe what is on the page. Talk about **why** the text has been designed in a particular way. What **effect** does each device have?

headline – grabs attention of reader

photos – show smiling people because they are happy in their work

bold introduction – to mark out the description of each person, before their actual words are given

pull-quote – stands out because (a) larger, (b) in orange. It highlights the actual words of each person interviewed.

block capitals – emphasise the people's names

overall design – text in columns, orange and black used

Q: Are we a nation of workaholics?

Workaholics can't make their minds up

MARKSTEEN ADAMSON, 40, is a founding partner of advertising agency ArthurSteenHorneAdamson (www.ashawebsite.com). He is married, has four children and lives in Cheltenham.
I worked for years in advertising

I work hard because I have no choice

IVANA STRUKIEL, 38, is single, a cleaner and lives in North London. Born in Poland, she moved to England two years ago. My stresses are not the stresses of a managing director in the City, but they are financial and physical: stooping down, straining my back, carrying heavy equipment every day. You have to make a lot of sacrifices just to survive in a city like London. The cost of living is very high and it's hard to find work. I would like to be an administrator or a translator but, because I have bills to pay, I am a cleaner. I work probably 45 hours a week and clean eight houses to be able to afford my lifestyle – which is a room in a shared household with many other people. I'm not complaining. It's OK, it is

Long hours don't produce better work

RACHEL OSAIGBOVO, 31, is co-director of the Festival of Youth Arts (www.festivalofyoutharts. org.uk). She lives in London with her partner.
You shouldn't need longer than nine-to-five to

Here is how one student commented on the way layout and presentational devices are used in the article:

> The article is designed in three columns because it gives three interviews. Two of them have photos, which show people who are not workaholics and so are happy with their jobs. Each column begins in the same way. First there is a quotation, to show the most important thing that the person thinks about the question. Then there is a paragraph in bold, which introduces the person and gives their name in capitals to make it stand out. Then their speech is given in ordinary 'look', as this is the main part of the article. The orange touches, which make the article feel "cheery", alongside the smiles in the pictures, make this an attractive piece of writing.

Grade C

Good Points

- The different presentational features are identified, even if the correct terms are not always used.
- The purpose of all the features is given.
- It includes an opinion about how effective the design is.

Question

Choose an article from your favourite magazine. List all the presentational devices used, and explain why they are used. How effective are they?

How to refer to the text successfully

Key points

- To support your answers, you need to **refer directly to the text**.
- The references should be **relevant** to the point you are making.
- Make **brief quotations** from the text, and **explain** what they show.

Quoting and referring

- Sometimes you may want to **quote** some words **directly** from the text. Put inverted commas around any words you quote. Include the quotation as part of your sentence:

  The writer emphasises how delicious the ice cream is. 'Mmmm'. ✘

  By placing 'Mmmm' in a paragraph of its own, the writer emphasises how delicious the ice cream is. ✔

- Sometimes you might want to identify a number of words to prove your point:

  The writer emphasises how delicious the cream is when she says: 'Mmmm. That was fantastic!'

- Each quotation should be relevant – you are quoting to **back up your own points**. Don't quote because you can't think of anything else to say!

- Try to add a **comment** about each quotation to **explain** why you have included it.

- Sometimes you may want simply to **refer to a detail** in the text, but not quote it directly. You can use your own words:

  The writer points out that no other ice cream has the same quality and price.

Look at this extract from *Africa Today*, and how the student analyses it.

> When she spoke to the conference, Celia Bowers was quite clear about what her department was going to do. She felt that in just two years' time people would notice the difference: the quality of water would be improved and, indeed, the places in which people lived would be transformed …

The writer makes Celia Bowers seem confident from the start. He says she 'was clear' about her objectives. This suggests she has thought through her ideas, and can put them across very well. He describes some of the improvements that are planned. He moves from the quality of the water to the complete transformation of the region. This shows how wide-ranging and effective her plans are.

Grade C

Good Points

- Either direct quotations or references to the text are used to support each point.
- Comments explain why the references have been made.

Top Tip!

Make sure you **read the question carefully** to see exactly what you have to do. You may be asked to read only part of a text. Notice helpful information, such as:
*Read the **opening paragraph** and explain …*
*Find **three facts** and say **how they support** what the writer believes …*
*What **techniques** are used **to convince** the reader that …*

Top Tip!

Try not to quote large amounts of text – it won't gain you marks.

Task

Improve the student's answer on page 19 by adding a quotation from the text. Make sure it is relevant, and that you add a comment which backs up your quotation.

Analysing text types

Key points

- There are **different kinds** of media and non-fiction texts, such as newspaper stories, websites and travel writing. These are called **text types**.

Page 6

- Each text type uses particular kinds of **language**, **layout** and **presentational features** to achieve its purpose.

- To get good marks, you need to show that you understand **how** and **why** these devices are used.

News reports

- The main purpose of news reports is to **give information**. Many also aim to **entertain**, especially stories.

Page 18

- Many **presentational devices** are used to attract the reader.

- **Key points** of the story are given first. Later paragraphs give more **detail** and include **quotations** from the people involved.

Look at this report from *The Sun*.

Strapline tells you more about the story.

Catchy **headline** put in capitals.

Picture shows ship looking old/ ready to scrap – lots of grey.

'Protest' shows the human interest, and suggests conflict.

Short paragraphs (one sentence each) make text easy to read.

'Toxic rust-bucket' – strong language makes ship sound dangerous.

'TOXIC' RUST-BUCKET IS HERE

Protest as ship docks

A RUSTING ghost ship dubbed a "toxic time bomb" arrives in Britain yesterday — to be greeted by crowds of angry environmental protesters.

The Caloosahatchee, one of four redundant US Navy vessels being sent here to be scrapped, docked at Hartlepool, Teesside.

Protesters say they are packed with toxic chemicals and must be returned to America.

The Government allowed the ships to dock in Hartlepool — but says the local firm that won the contract to scrap them must not start until a legal row over their fate is decided.

Protester Barbara Crosbie, 36, from Hartlepool said yesterday: "Ninety per cent of people living here don't think this is right. We're angry and want all these ships sent back."

First paragraph sums up the story.

Later paragraphs give more background and detail.

Final paragraph is a **quotation** from an eye-witness, for human interest.

Text box makes report stand out.

People give scale and show it's a human story as well.

Web pages

- Web pages have a variety of purposes, but often **sell** products or give **information**.
- **Design** is an important feature – web pages have to **attract** the reader.
- **Text**: writing has to be **brief** and **punchy**, as readers have a short attention span as they surf the net.

main heading to show what this page is about: the holiday section of 'lifestyle'

main image to attract attention: suggests fabulous foreign holiday

commands to get reader to click on text: 'get inspiration', etc.

name of website provider

search button

main navigation bar with links to other content

questions to grab reader's attention: 'What's your holiday money worth?' etc.

active links in green (matching colour of main photo)

short snatches of text to tempt the reader in for more

logo stands out

pictures show variety of content and are attractive

wordplay (lots of 'v's) to amuse/attract reader

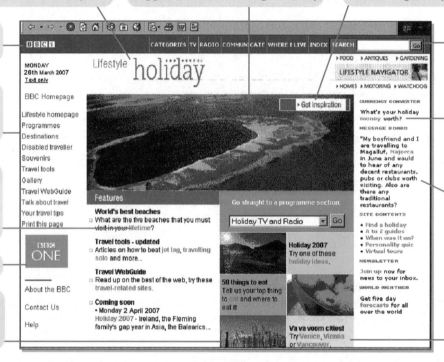

Here is one student's analysis of this web page:

This web page is designed to interest people thinking about a holiday. So it gives lots of information about different places, and pictures to attract the reader. The main picture makes you go 'Wow' and will attract any traveller, there are also some smaller pictures which show other places to go to and things to do.

The text is written to attract the reader as well. Phrases like 'Try ...', 'Tell us ...' aim to get the reader to do things. There are quite a lot of questions as well, such as 'What's your holiday money worth?' These speak directly to the reader and make them want to answer the question by reading further. Finally there is also some 'fun' writing, like 'Va va voom cities' which is another way of keeping the reader's interest.

The website is organised so that people can find their way about the site easily. There is a navigation bar on the left, and lots of links everywhere to other pages. The link text is in green to make it stand out. Above all, there aren't any long bits of writing, as readers don't have time for this. Instead lots of headings are given (like 'World's best beaches') and the first bits of text, just to give readers the flavour of the full articles. It's teasing them really, but very effective.

Grade C

Good Points

- The answer covers the language, images and the overall presentation.
- It takes into account the purpose and the audience of the website.
- It refers to relevant details from the text to back up the points made.

Top Tip!

Whenever you analyse or discuss a media text, you are likely to have to cover two main areas in your answer:

– **language**: content, style and organisation

– **presentational devices**: photos, graphics, bullet points, colour, etc.

Autobiographies

- You may be given an extract from some **travel writing**, or an account of someone's life (**biography/autobiography**).

- This kind of non-fiction does not use presentational devices, so your focus must be on the **language**.

- Sometimes the text is **telling a story**, so think about the way the story builds up, and what the characters say and do.

This extract is from an **autobiography** by Sir Robin Day. Sir Robin used to interview politicians on television. Here, he describes his first ever time in front of the cameras. This was in the 1950s, when television was not so hi-tech!

Short sentences at start – makes the story dramatic.

Building tension – he is sweating from anxiety as well as heat.

Spoken dialogue, as in a story – adds interest and variety.

Countdown – adds tension.

Describing detail – brings scene to life.

effective language – contrast of 'crisp and bright', then 'limp and dull'

short sentence – dramatic ending

I was ready to go. But there was a little more delay. The lighting was causing trouble with my spectacles – reflection flashes from the lenses and shadows from the heavy hornrims. An engineer climbed up ladders to adjust the arc-lamps until the director in the control room was satisfied. It seemed to take a very long time. I began to sweat under the heat of the lights.

We had been asked to memorise our material so that we would not have to look down. They wanted to see us looking full-face into the camera. I took a final look at my notes. The phrases which last night were crisp and bright seemed limp and dull, but it was too late to make any changes.

'Are you ready?' called the floor manager. I nodded.

'Stand by.' He stood to one side of the camera, and raised his arm above his shoulder.

'Thirty seconds to go ... Fifteen seconds.'

Suddenly the floor-manager jabbed his hand down towards me. A red light glowed on top of the camera. This was it.

Here is one way to start analysing the language used in the extract:

Grade C

Robin Day is describing what he had to cope with when he presented a TV programme. He writes in a dramatic way. For example, he begins with a short sentence, which makes it seem tense, as if he is taking short breaths ...

The problems with the glasses and the lights are mentioned to show how everything seems to be going wrong, making Sir Robin more worried (he says 'I began to sweat ...', which isn't just from the heat in the studio). He tries to remember his lines, but 'The phrases ... seemed limp and dull'. Obviously, it is all building up inside him, and he thinks there is going to be a disaster. The countdown adds to the tension. The final short sentence is like a 'lift-off'. It makes you want to read on to see if it was OK.

Good Points

- The student analyses in detail how the writer tells a good story.
- The use of language is always central to the answer.
- The purpose of this part of the text is taken into account.
- Relevant quotations are used to support the ideas.

Task

Write two paragraphs analysing the newspaper report on page 21. Comment on:
- the language
- the image and presentational devices.

Comparing texts

Key points

- One question will probably ask you to **compare two texts**. This means saying what is **similar** and/or **different** about the texts.

- The question should make it clear **which features of the texts are to be compared**.

- You need to **refer to both texts** in your answer, and link the texts.

Providing the right details

- Read the question carefully to make sure that you provide the **right information**. The wording of the question will show you exactly what you should be comparing in the texts. For example:

> Which text is more successful?
> Compare the texts by writing about how the writers have used:
>   - fact and opinion
>   - argument.

The **main question**, which asks you to compare the texts. The focus of your answer should be on how **successful** they are.

The **bullet points** list the particular features you must analyse – the writers' use of fact and opinion, and argument. You need to comment on how successful these features are, and say which works better in each text, and why.

Organising your answer

- You could discuss Text 1, then Text 2, and sum up how they are similar and/or different at the end, in a final paragraph. This is a straightforward approach, but it doesn't allow you to compare the texts until the end of your answer.

- Better is to take each point (bullet point) at a time, and compare both texts together.

- Begin a new paragraph each time you deal with a new point.

- End with a short paragraph that sums up your answer.

For example, you could structure your answer to the question above like this:

Para 1 - short introduction covering both texts, e.g. their purpose and audience
Para 2 - discuss use of fact and opinion in Text 1 and Text 2
Para 3 - discuss use of argument in Text 1 and Text 2
Para 4 - short conclusion referring back to main question: which text is more successful?

Linking the texts

- When you refer to the texts, you must clearly **link one text to the other**. This means using a linking word or phrase, e.g.

  The first text concentrates on giving advice to old people. However, the second text ...

- Use some of the words and phrases on the right to make your comparisons clear:

when texts are similar	when texts are different
similarly	in contrast
just as ... , so ...	whereas
likewise	on the other hand
also	but
	however

Two texts to compare

Compare these texts.
Write about:
- how they appeal to their audience
- the use of language.

Text 1

This is from a teachers' newspaper. It is about an old teacher called Charles Crossley, describing his life and achievements.

In his first teaching post at Loveridge Primary School, Crossley discovered by accident the power of poetry to keep unruly eight and nine-year-olds in order.

'I used to have a huge class of 50 or 60 boys every Friday afternoon,' he said. 'I was never properly prepared for the lesson, and they used to turn me into a nervous wreck. One Friday I opened a book of my poems in desperation and just read to them.'

The boys were transfixed, and from then on were putty in his hands. 'They simply seemed to love the experience,' he said.

Text 2

This article from a local newspaper offers a different view of young people.

Pensioner's life made a misery by 'young vandals'

Frank Blackburn, 78, who lives on the Albany Estate, has been a prisoner in his house each evening for over a year. Groups of children, many as young as 7 or 8, have made him fear for his life and the safety of his property.

Gangs

Stones have been thrown through his windows, excrement has been pushed through his letter box and he cannot sleep. Gangs roam the area, shouting and drinking. Other older residents are just as fearful.

'The thugs gather every night,' says Frank. 'The police don't do anything about it.'

You could begin your answer like this:

Grade C

Begins by giving a general statement about the language in the extracts.

A personal response – if you can back up your opinion, this will gain you extra marks.

'however' makes a clear comparison with the first text.

The language of the two texts is very different. In the first extract the language makes Crossley seems like an inspiring teacher: 'he discovered ... the power'. It is even a bit exaggerated – I can't imagine the boys being 'transfixed' and like putty, though it was the old days. In the second text, however, the language is unpleasant: 'misery', 'thugs'. Frank is a 'prisoner' in his own house. The estate is rough, full of 'stones', 'excrement', 'gangs' and fear. The final statement from Frank is that the police do nothing. This makes us sympathise with the old people even more.

This difference is partly because the first article is looking back over someone's life and celebrating it, so the language is blown up a bit to make the teacher seem wonderful. Other teachers will like reading about this. Whereas the description of the estate in the other article is very upsetting and modern – which is what the writer intended.

This shows that the student is focusing on one extract first.

This shows that the student is now moving on to talk about the second text.

Brief quotations are used which are relevant to the points being made.

In this paragraph the student looks at the two texts together, and gives a reason why their language is different.

Task

Compare the two texts above by writing about their use of fact and opinion. Refer to the audience of each text in your answer.

Raising your grade

If you want to raise your grade to C or above, you need to show these skills.

Answer all parts of the question

- Read the question **carefully** and answer it **exactly**.
- If it asks you to comment on only part of a text, then don't comment on all of it.
- If it asks you to comment on the language used, then don't comment on the presentational devices.
- If **bullet point** 'prompts' are given, use them to structure your answer.

Show that you understand the text

- Think about the **type** of text that it is (biography? newspaper article? etc.) and refer to this in your answer.
- Think about **why** the text has been written (its **purpose**) and **who** it is written for (the **audience**).
- Talking about the text in this way shows that you **understand** it. For example:

  The writer seems to be addressing ordinary people. We know this because he uses short sentences and simple words. There are lots of illustrations, which would appeal to someone just glancing through the newspaper rather than spending ages reading it.

Comment on the text, don't just describe it

- The examiner doesn't want to know what is in the text, but about how **effects** are created.
- This means thinking about the **writer's techniques**, not just the content.
- Give **your opinion** about how effective you think certain features are.

  After lots of long sentences there is suddenly a short sentence, 'No good'. ✘

  After lots of long sentences there is suddenly a short sentence: 'No good'. <u>This shows how the runaway has come to the end of the road and has nowhere to turn. The reader stops, just like he does.</u> ✔

Refer to the texts in your answer

- Give **evidence** for your ideas by **quoting** from the text.
- Choose **brief** quotations and make sure they are **relevant** to the point you are making.
- Quote the words **exactly**, and put them in **inverted commas** ('…'). Or refer to the text by **summarising**.
- Give a **comment** which explains why you are quoting from the text.

  The writer presents himself as a pathetic figure: <u>he 'waves feebly at the taxi then steps away quickly as it races past him, covering him with muddy water'.</u> ✘

  The writer presents himself as a pathetic figure who <u>'waves feebly' at the taxi then gets splashed as it races past him.</u> This makes us laugh at him, but also feel a bit sorry for him.

Read the question and the student's answer below. The notes show why the examiner awarded it a C grade.

What impression of Nivea for Men is this advertisement trying to create?
In your answer, explain:
- the use of language
- the use of layout and presentational devices.

THEY'VE RUN OUT OF HALF-TIME PIES.

Life has enough irritations. Don't let your skin be one of them.
NIVEA FOR MEN® Extra Soothing Moisturiser soothes and calms your skin.

Grade C

The advertisement is funny because it's advertising some products for skin care but the eye-catching writing makes you think it could be about pies. So the idea is that you want to know what on earth this has got to do with anything. And of course it fits the reader who is a man because they will know all about watching the match and not being able to get pies at half time.

> Tries to show an understanding of the main feature of the advert, though the expression is a bit unclear.

The smaller writing at the bottom explains what it's all about. The 'irritation' joke is a good one because there are two meanings of irritation being used, skin irritation and annoyance. Humour is a good way of selling something. Also, the advertiser talks directly to the user – 'your skin'. This is another good technique because it makes the reader think they are being targeted.

> Good reference to the text – the student doesn't have to quote all the text but just puts the key word in inverted commas.

The capitals look strong and manly like the person buying the product. Capitals are used for the name of the product at the bottom as well – in that case, because it's important. Otherwise it's interesting that the actual name of the product doesn't take up much space – though it's on the picture of the cream of course, so that we recognise it.

> Another thoughtful comment – the student isn't just describing the text.

Most of the advertisement is blue, and blue is 'for a boy', so this is appropriate for men. The actual product is shown on the right of the advert. It looks straightforward, not flashy, and again, this will appeal to an average man who might not want to buy a beauty product.

> Another reference to the purpose and audience of the text.

> The student shows an awareness of how the audience is being targeted.

> Comments on the effect of the techniques.

> Student moves on here to discuss the design features – s/he has used the bullet points in the question well to structure the answer. This helps the student to answer all parts of the question.

Paper 2 Section A: Reading poems from different cultures and traditions

Key points

- Paper 2 Section A will focus on poems from different cultures and traditions. You have been reading these poems from your Anthology in class.

- There will be two questions, but you will only have to answer one of them. The question will ask you to compare one named poem with another poem of your choice.

- One question will target the first eight poems in the Anthology – Cluster 1. The other question will target the second eight poems – Cluster 2.

- This section of the exam counts for 15% of your total mark.

- You will spend about 45 minutes on your answer.

Top Tip!
Focus on your reading skills when answering the Reading questions. You won't get any marks for your spelling, punctuation and grammar.

The exam paper

Paper 2 has two sections. Section A is Reading Poetry. Section B is Writing to inform, explain, describe. Only Section A of the exam paper is given here.

Paper 1 Section A: Foundation Tier

READING: POEMS FROM DIFFERENT CULTURES AND TRADITIONS

Answer one question.

You are allowed to refer to a copy of the Anthology in the examination.

You are given two questions, and you have to answer one of them.

You will be given a clean copy of the Anthology in the exam. You can't refer to your own marked-up copy.

EITHER

Question 1 focuses on the 1st Cluster of poems in the Anthology. One poem is named and you choose another one to compare it with.

1 Compare *Night of the Scorpion* with any other poem of your choice. How do the poets present relationships in the poems?

Remember to:
- compare the poems
- write about relationships in the poems
- say how the relationships have been presented. *(27 marks)*

The bullet points list the things you must write about. Make sure you cover all these in your answer.

OR

Question 2 focuses on the 2nd Cluster of poems in the Anthology. One poem is named and you choose another one to compare it with.

2 How is language used to reveal the speaker's situation in *Not My Business* and in any other poem of your choice?

Remember to:
- write about the language used in the poems
- write about the speakers' situations
- deal with two poems. *(27 marks)*

The skills you will be assessed on

The questions that you are asked in Paper 2 Section A test certain reading skills. This table outlines the skills that are tested (on the left), and explains what you have to do to get good marks (on the right).

The skill you need to show	How to get good marks
1 Understanding what the texts are about *Pages 30–47*	• Know and explain **what the poems are about**. • Think about the **meaning** of the poem. Often there are **deeper meanings** hiding under the obvious meaning. • Understand **why** the poems have been written. What is the **purpose** of the poet in writing it?
2 Referring to the texts in your answer *Pages 30–47*	• **Refer to the poems** in your answer, to provide evidence for your views. • This includes the use of **quotations**. • The references to the poems must be **relevant** to the point you are making.
3 Understanding the techniques that writers use *Pages 36–47*	• Show where the writers have used language to **create an effect**, e.g. powerful words or images. • Explain **why** these techniques have been used, and **how effective** they are. • Write about the **structure** of the poem, such as how it begins, develops and ends. • Describe the **way it is set out on the page**, e.g. the lengths of the lines or stanzas (verses).
4 Choosing the right information and comparing texts *Pages 32–47*	• **Select the right information** from the poems to answer the question, e.g. by skimming or scanning. • Write about the ways in which the poems are **similar or different**. • **Refer to examples** across both poems.

Question

It always helps to revise poems in pairs, since you have to compare two poems in the exam itself. Look at these lists. Which two poems from the list on the right would you use to answer each question, and why?

Question	Poems
A question about suffering	*Nothing's Changed*
A question about poverty	*Limbo*
A question about inequality	*Island Man*
A question about Man and Nature	*Night of the Scorpion*
A question about contrasting cultures	*What Were They Like?*
	Two Scavengers in a Truck...
	Blessing
	Vultures

Different cultures and traditions

Key points

- The poems in the Anthology all deal with **different cultures or traditions**.

- **Culture** refers to the ideas, beliefs and way of life of a particular race, country, religion or social group.

- **Traditions** are the customs that are commonly followed by people in a culture.

- The cultures and traditions are revealed by the **language** that is used, the **setting**, the **people**, and their **situations** and **problems**.

- You need to show that you **understand how** the poems reflect these different cultures and traditions.

Language

- In all the Anthology poems, language plays a big part in setting the poem within a particular culture.

  - It can show how people speak:

    munay hutoo kay aakhee jeebh aakhee bhasha

    (*from Search For My Tongue* by Sujata Bhatt)

    Explain yuself
    wha yu mean

    (*Half-Caste* by John Agard)

  - It gives us names: Oya, Shango and Hattie (*Hurricane Hits England*).

  - It mentions items unfamiliar to many people in Britain, e.g. yams in *Not My Business*; a salwar kameez in *Presents from my Aunts in Pakistan*; paddies and water buffalo in *What Were They Like?*

- It is very important to show that you understand **how** the poets use language, and **why**.

Look at this extract from a Grade C answer about the language used in *from Unrelated Incidents*.

Describes what the poem is doing.

Explains the poet's use of language.

Gives an example from the poem to back up the point.

The comment shows exactly how the use of language creates an effect.

Grade C

In 'from Unrelated Incidents', Tom Leonard is criticising BBC English and all it represents. He does this by using a Scottish accent - the words are spelt in this accent to show they are spoken differently, for example 'wia' instead of 'with a'. This makes the newsreader seem like an ordinary person, not someone with a posh accent. Even though the newsreader suggests that Scottish people are rough ('wanna yoo scruff'), we wonder whether they are more honest than people who put on an accent like on the BBC.

Shows the reaction of the readers to the use of language.

thi reason
a talk wia
BBC accent
iz coz yi
widny wahnt
mi ti talk
aboot thi
trooth wia
voice lik
wanna yoo
scruff...
yooz doant no
thi trooth
yirsellz cawz
yi canny talk
right.
(*from Unrelated Incidents*)

People and settings

Top Tip!

When revising the poems, note the key words which tell the reader what is special or different about the people, the place or their beliefs.

You can quote these words if they are relevant to the question you are answering.

The key words are underlined in the examples on this page.

The poets might write about people and places that are different from those we find in Britain. For example:

peasants; their life
was in rice and bamboo.

    (*What Were They Like?* by Denise Levertov)

a bright yellow garbage truck
   with two garbagemen in red plastic blazers
standing on the back stoop…

    (*Two Scavengers in a Truck, Two Beautiful People in a Mercedes* by Lawrence Ferlinghetti)

This poem is set in America. It is closer to our own world, but still different.

Situations and problems

The poets often write about problems that come from being in a different culture:

- **Being away from home**

  In *Island Man*, by Grace Nichols, the central character has left his island home and is now coping with life in a huge city. He has to drag himself out of bed to face the day:

  island man heaves himself
  Another London day

  The phrase 'another London day' makes his life seem heavy and depressing.

- **Slavery**

  In *Limbo*, Kamau Brathwaite describes the terrible suffering of the African slaves:

      stick is the whip
    and the dark deck is slavery

  The ending, though, suggests there might be hope of some kind:

      and the music is saving me.

- **Endless evil**

  Some poems are very dark, and seem to offer no hope:

  Vultures, by Chinua Achebe, is about 'the perpetuity of evil' – there is always going to be evil in the world, because of human nature.

  Nothing's Changed, by Tatamkhula Afrika argues that there are still divisions between blacks and whites in South Africa.

- **The struggle for existence**

  In many poems, people just have to struggle on:

  In *Night of the Scorpion*, Nissim Ezekiel describes his mother's suffering. The neighbours cannot help her, but rely on prayer and superstition.

- **Hope for the future**

  Sometimes there are some flashes of hope:

  In *This Room*, Imtiaz Dharker describes a sense of joy and excitement:

  This is the time and place
  to be alive.

Task

Compare the way of life presented in *Two Scavengers from a Truck, Two Beautiful People in a Mercedes* with the way of life presented in any other poem of your choice from the Anthology.

Write about:
- what we learn of the people
- the kind of society in which they live
- how language is used by the poets.

Content, message and attitude

Key points

- When you write about poems from different cultures and traditions, you may have to comment on:
  - the **content** of the poems
  - the **messages** in the poems
  - the poets' **attitudes** to the subject.

What the poem is saying

- For each of the poems you are studying, you need to understand exactly **what the poem is about**. Ask yourself these questions: who? what? where? when? why?

These notes on the opening of *Vultures* by Chinua Achebe pick out the basic facts – what is going on in the poem.

A dawn scene is described.

A vulture sits in a tree.

The vulture nestles up to his mate. Its physical appearance is described.

They ate a corpse earlier on.

They sit on a branch after eating and watch the remains.

> In the greyness
> and drizzle of one despondent
> dawn unstirred by harbingers
> of sunbreak a vulture
> perching high on broken
> bone of a dead tree
> nestled close to his
> mate his smooth
> bashed-in head, a pebble
> on a stem rooted in
> a dump of gross
> feathers, inclined affectionately
> to hers. Yesterday they picked
> the eyes of a swollen
> corpse in a water-logged
> trench and ate the
> things in its bowel. Full
> gorged they chose their roost
> keeping the hallowed remnant
> in easy range of cold
> telescopic eyes...

Top Tip!

When you write about a poem, you need to go deeper than the obvious surface meaning. Often the language will give you a clue as to the poet's meaning. For example:

The tree is 'dead' and the branch is described as a 'broken bone'. These are both images of death, which suit the fact that vultures are being described. The poet is telling us from the start that he is talking about death.

Going deeper: the meaning of the poem

- On a second reading of the poem, try to go deeper than understanding the bare facts. What **meaning** does the poet give to the bare details?

- Look closely at the **language** and **tone**. They give some clues to the meaning.

Here is the opening of *Vultures* again. This time the comments show the **meaning** of the individual details.

> In the greyness
> and drizzle of one despondent
> dawn unstirred by harbingers
> of sunbreak a vulture
> perching high on broken
> bone of a dead tree
> nestled close to his
> mate his smooth
> bashed-in head, a pebble
> on a stem rooted in
> a dump of gross
> feathers, inclined affectionately
> to hers. Yesterday they picked
> the eyes of a swollen
> corpse in a water-logged
> trench and ate the
> things in its bowel. Full
> gorged they chose their roost
> keeping the hallowed remnant
> in easy range of cold
> telescopic eyes...

It's a depressing scene, which sets the tone for the poem.

'broken bone' and 'dead tree' are images of death.

The 'affection' is surprising for birds described as so ugly.

Gruesome details – we feel disgusted.

The description of their eyes makes them seem hard and unfeeling.

The message of the poem

- Poems always have a **message**. This might be a general observation about life, or it might be about rights and wrongs.

- In these poems, the message is often about the different culture.

- The message is not given openly – instead we slowly come to understand it the more we read the poem.

- You can often work out the message by moving from the **specific example(s)** described in the poem to a **general statement**:

Poem	Specific example(s) from the poem	General statement/message
Vultures	• Vultures can love in the midst of death. • Concentration camp commandant is evil but kind to his child.	• It is strange how all creatures, including humans, are a mix of good and evil.
Island Man	• A man from the Caribbean wakes in London but has images from his homeland.	• People who move from one culture to another are often torn between the two places.
Nothing's Changed	• District Six in Cape Town – the division between whites and blacks.	• Even after the end of Apartheid, there is division between whites and blacks, rich and poor.
from Unrelated Incidents	• Newsreader is talking in a Scottish accent, explaining that this could make him sound unbelievable to those who speak more 'correct' English.	• When people speak in non-standard English they are looked down on, but actually speaking in a 'posh' accent is false.
Not My Business	• Three people are 'disappeared' by people in power – the speaker doesn't help them, but then he too is taken away.	• Unless people help others in a violent society, everyone will suffer.

Commenting on meaning and message

- Remember to refer to the **language** of the poem to back up your comments.

This is how you could analyse lines 1–29 of Vultures:

The vultures are described in detail by the poet. They are described as ugly to look at, the male with a 'bashed-in head'. They have 'cold telescopic' eyes, which makes them frightening. The whole scene is a bit depressing: 'drizzle' and 'despondent'.

This is because death is part of the description. Although the birds are affectionate to each other, they have been eating a corpse, including its bowel – horrible details which make them even more frightening.

The next section makes a general comment – the poet says it's strange how those in love can ignore horrible things around them. The idea of falling asleep in a 'charnel-house' is powerful, because a charnel-house is like an abattoir.

Grade C

Good Points

- The student goes beyond the factual meaning of the poem to discuss the underlying meaning.
- References to the language are used to show the meaning.
- All the ideas are supported with details from the text.
- There are three clear sections: the birds, their behaviour and the general point (the message).

The poet's attitude to the subject

- You might be asked to comment on **the poet's own feelings** about the situation in the poems.

- You can often work out these feelings by studying the **language** the poet uses.

- These notes show how Niyi Osundare's attitude is clear from the start in *Not My Business*. We are shown what is happening in the society and how people react to it. People ignore the suffering of others and think only of themselves.

Top Tip!

- If the poet writes in the first person (using 'I') she or he may sometimes be talking about their own views, or their own experience.
- However, the poet may well be 'hiding' behind another personality to make their point. Here, the 'I' in *Not My Business* represents the person who is just standing by. Niyi Osundare is attacking this attitude.

'stuffed' suggests rough treatment, 'belly' suggests they fed him to an animal or monster – another frightening image.

> They picked Akanni up one morning
> Beat him soft like clay
> And stuffed him down the belly
> Of a waiting jeep.
>   What business of mine is it
>   So long they don't take the yam
>   From my savouring mouth?

The simile ('like clay') shows that Akanni was beaten to a pulp. This is reinforced by the word 'soft', which also implies he was powerless.

The speaker's actual words are quoted. It is clear that he doesn't want to be involved. 'Savouring' suggests that he is only worried about his own satisfaction.

However, the fact that the speaker has tried not to get involved does not save him. His turn comes too:

He is frozen with fear – just as others have been fearful.

> And then one evening
> As I sat down to eat my yam
> A knock on the door froze my hungry hand.
> The jeep was waiting on my bewildered lawn
> Waiting, waiting in its usual silence.

He was more interested in his yams than in his neighbours' problems.

He is bewildered – how could this happen to him?

'usual silence' emphasises how everyone has been silent about the arrests.

- Sometimes the poet's attitude may be unclear, because he or she has mixed feelings. In *Vultures*, for example, the poet ends by saying:

    Praise bounteous providence ...

(We could praise because there is love even in an ogre.)

    or else *despair* ...

(We could despair because there is evil even in the 'germ' of love.)

We are left to make up our own minds.

Writing about attitude and message

- When you are writing about the poet's attitude or message you must **explain exactly what you mean**.

- You must also **support your comments** by referring closely to the poem.

In this example, a student was asked:

- to explain the poet's attitude to what happens in *Not My Business*
- to say what the reader can learn from the poem.

Starts with a general comment about the subject of the poem and how it is structured. This is one of the ways the poet shows his attitude, by making a contrast.

Explains how we are meant to be sympathetic to the victims, and critical of the speaker for doing nothing.

Grade C

From the start, the poem shows a contrast between someone being picked up by the police or the army, and then someone else saying how it is not their business. The three lines at the end of each stanza are from this other person who just stands by, doing nothing.

The poet makes it clear that there is suffering. For example, he uses names (Akanni, Danladi and Chinwe), which makes them seem like real people he knows. The detail also backs this up - Akanni, for instance, is beaten 'soft like clay', and when they come for Danladi, they 'booted the whole house awake'. The language is violent like the scene. There is also a mystery, for example Chinwe's job is taken for no clear reason and this is frightening.

So we are meant to be sympathetic to the people disappearing. But the other person continues to eat yams and look after himself. He is presented in a bad way, which is odd because he is the speaker in the poem, but we must remember that doesn't always mean he is the poet. In fact, it is clear that the poet is criticising him, as I have said.

In the end, the poet shows us that hoping to avoid trouble does not help anyone escape from oppression. This is the real message of the poem. He does this by showing how the speaker himself is picked up. The 'knock on the door' at the end is terrifying and even stops the speaker eating. This is where his silence led: to the jeep waiting on the lawn.

Detail about how the language of the poem presents the poet's attitude: real people are involved, real violence, and frightening mystery.

Explains the message of the poem.

Top Tip!

If you want to analyse the poet's attitude or message, ask yourself these questions:
- **What** is being said?
- **How** is it presented?
- **Why** is it presented in that way?

Question

Read *Blessing* by Imtiaz Dharker.
- What happens in the poem?
- What is the poet's attitude to it?
- What message can we take from the poem and in what way is it different from the message in *Not My Business*?

Structure

- You could be asked about the **structure** of the poems.

- This means analysing how each poem is **organised**: how it opens, develops and concludes.

- It also means analysing how each poem is **set out on the page**.

How the poem is organised

- Lawrence Ferlinghetti's *Two Scavengers in a Truck, Two Beautiful People in a Mercedes* could be broken into five sections:

lines 1–9	a description of the truck and the Mercedes caught together at the stoplight
lines 10–15	the 'elegant' couple in the Mercedes are described
lines 16–25	the 'grungy' couple in the garbage truck are described
lines 26–30	the 'scavengers' looking down at the couple
lines 31–37	message: they are close yet far apart.

  Note how this structure helps to organise the poet's ideas. We are led from step to step, ending with the poet's thoughts (the message).

- In contrast, *Night of the Scorpion* by Nissim Ezekiel is a **narrative**. The poem describes what happens to Ezekiel's mother over 20 hours. It tells:

  - what the scorpion did

  - how the neighbours react

  - how the incident is given a religious significance (*May the poison purify your flesh*)

  - the father's efforts to cure her

  - what his mother says at the end.

Structural devices

The poems in the Anthology use a variety of **structural devices**.
Look out for these when you comment on structure:

- **refrain** – a repeated chorus

  The refrain in *Limbo* suggests a kind of performance, as in a limbo dance:

  > *limbo*
  > *limbo like me*

- **stanza** – a fixed number of lines arranged in a pattern

  In *Not My Business*, the stanzas break into two parts: the first four lines tell what is happening to others, the final three lines tell how the speaker is reacting:

  > *They came one night*
  > *Booted the whole house awake*
  > *And dragged Danladi out,*
  > *Then off to a lengthy absence.*
  >   *What business of mine is it*
  >   *So long they don't take the yam*
  >   *From my savouring mouth?*

- **repetition** – of words or phrases

  Half-Caste uses repetition to challenge the listener's or reader's views about 'half-castes':

  > *Explain yuself*
  > *wha yu mean.*

- **pattern** – a repeated movement that gives shape to the poem.

  Vultures has:

  – a stanza about the birds, followed by a stanza with a general statement about what this means.

  – a stanza about the Commandant, followed by a stanza with a general statement, which links the birds and the man.

How the poem is presented

- The **different line lengths and indentations** which are a feature of Lawrence Ferlinghetti's *Two Scavengers in a Truck, Two Beautiful People in a Mercedes* suggest the movement in the travellers' lives:

> At the stoplight waiting for the light
>   nine a.m. downtown San Francisco
> a bright yellow garbage truck
>   with two garbagemen in red plastic blazers
> standing on the back stoop
>   one on each side hanging on
> and looking down into
>   an elegant open Mercedes
> with an elegant couple in it

> There is no punctuation at the end of lines, so the sentence runs on. The effect is to suggest this is a 'slice of life' that doesn't begin or end – it is endless.

- Later, the lines on the page may even suggest the sea's movement:

>   across that small gulf
>   in the high seas
>   of this democracy.

If you had to comment on the layout of this poem, you could write:

> The poem gives the impression of someone speaking. Their pauses might be the breaks in the lines. It looks random, but sometimes the position of the words on the lines makes sense:
> 'and looking down into
>   an elegant open Mercedes
>   with an elegant couple in it'.
> In this extract the reader's eye drops to the next line, like the garbagemen looking down at the car.

Note how the layout is **explained**, rather than just identified: 'The reader drops to the next line ...'

- The layout of *Night of the Scorpion* is **solid blocks of text**. This suits a narrative poem. The mother's words are contained in their own short stanza at the end to emphasise their significance:

> My mother only said
> Thank God the scorpion picked on me
> and spared my children.

- The **shape of the lines** in *Limbo* conveys the movements of the limbo dancers:

> knees spread wide
> and the dark ground is under me
>
> down
> down
> down

Question

Read *What Were They Like?* by Denise Levertov.
- How is the poem structured?
- Why has it been structured in this way?
- How successful is this structure?

Language

- You will always have to write about the **language** in the poems.

- You need to comment on **poetic techniques** (e.g. similes, rhyme and rhythm) and **language use** (how the poet uses words, sentences and punctuation).

- You will also need to **explain what effect** the language has on the reader.

Poetic techniques

- **Similes** are comparisons using 'like' or 'as':

    The peasants came like swarms of flies
        (Night of the Scorpion)

Comparing the peasants to flies makes them seem irritating, like pests.

- **Metaphors** are direct comparisons – giving something the qualities of something else:

    the bud opens, the bud opens in my mouth
        (from Search for My Tongue)

The new tongue is described as a flower that blossoms in the speaker's mouth.

- **Symbols** are objects that stand for a general idea:

In *from Search for My Tongue*, the idea of being caught between two languages and two cultures is symbolised by the two tongues that grow in the speaker's mouth.

- **Rhythm** is the beat of the poem – the pattern made by the sounds of the words:

    he always comes back   groggily groggily
    Comes back to sands
        (Island Man)

The rhythm suggests the beating of the waves on the shore.

- **Rhyme** is when words end with the same sound. The words could be at the ends of lines (as below), or within the lines:

    when the daily furniture of our lives
    stirs, when the improbable arrives.
        (This Room)

The rhyme emphasises those words.

- **Repetition** means using the same words or groups of words:

    but yu must come back tomorrow
    wid de whole of yu eye
    an de whole of yu ear
    an de whole of yu mind
        (Half-Caste)

The repetition emphasises how people who say 'half-caste' are not looking at the whole picture.

- **Alliteration** is when words that are close together begin with the same letter:

    Brash with glass,
    name flaring like a flag
        (Nothing's Changed)

The repeated 'fl' sound emphasises the name of the whites only inn, as if it is fluttering in the speaker's face.

- **Assonance** is when the same vowel sounds are repeated:

> What is the meaning of trees ...
> Their cratered graves?
> > (Hurricane Hits England)

The 'ee' sound is repeated in the first line, and the 'ay' sound in the second line. These sounds may suggest the sounds of the hurricane.

- Sometimes the sound of the words represents the sound of the action being described (this is called **onomatopoeia**):

> Imagine the drip of it,
> the small splash, echo
> in a tin mug
> > (Blessing)

The poet represents the drip and the splash by the words she uses.

- You need to do more than just **name** the poetic techniques. The examiner is looking for an **explanation** of why they have been used and the **effect** they are creating.

And limbo stick is the silence in front of me
limbo

limbo
limbo like me
limbo
limbo like me

long dark night is the silence in front of me
limbo
limbo like me

stick hit sound
and the ship like it ready

stick hit sound
and the dark still steady

limbo
limbo like me

long dark deck and the water surrounding me
long dark deck and the silence is over me

limbo
limbo like me

stick is the whip
and the dark deck is slavery

stick is the whip
and the dark deck is slavery

limbo
limbo like me

drum stick knock
and the darkness is over me

If you were analysing the poetic techniques used in *Limbo*, you could write this:

'Limbo' is an attempt to show the suffering of the African slaves as they are transported to America. So the rhyme and rhythm of the poem suggests the limbo dance, and maybe also the slaves dancing and chanting on the ship. For example, there is a repeated 'chorus', like the chorus of a song:
'limbo
limbo like me'.
The repetition in the poem adds to the effect of a dance or song, such as 'and the ship like it ready ... and the dark still steady'. You can almost imagine the slaves stamping their feet – or the audience clapping the limbo dancers.
The poem is also very symbolic. The 'stick' is a limbo stick, but also represents the way in which the slaves are beaten. The stick is their master. The 'dark deck' stands for their slavery, the darkness shows that light and joy have gone from their lives. The alliteration of 'd's emphasises this idea.

Grade C

Describes the purpose of the poem and links it to techniques. All poetic effects have a purpose.

Gives an example, and explains that it is used to suggest a song.

Names the technique (repetition), gives an example, and explains its effect.

Names the technique (symbolism) and gives a detailed example.

Other language use

You need to identify where particular **words**, **sentences** or **punctuation** (commas, full stops, etc.) have been used for effect. These language features will have been chosen by the poet to give meaning to the poem.

- Individual words might create a **particular effect**:

    My mother cherished her jewellery –
    Indian gold, dangling, filigree.
        (Presents from my Aunts in Pakistan)

    The detailed description of the jewellery, especially the unusual word 'filigree', makes it seem foreign and fascinating.

- Some words may have **associations**, making the reader think of something else, which adds meaning:

    fumes of human roast
        (Vultures)

    'Roast' suggests a meal, which makes the image of human death even more disgusting. It also links back to the vultures' meal.

- Note the **length of the sentences**:

    In *Blessing* by Imtiaz Dharker, the sentences get longer and longer. This contrasts the dryness of drought with the flood of water when the pipe bursts.

- Look closely at the **punctuation** as well:

    Island Man has no punctuation other than capital letters. This suggests the dreamlike state the man is in.

- The **position** of the words on the line can be important:

    This is the time and place
    to be alive
        (This Room)

    Putting 'to be alive' on its own line suggests this is a key idea in the poem.

- These notes show how Derek Walcott has used language in *Love After Love*:

'own' is repeated to emphasise 'yourself'. (Central idea of poem is coming to terms with yourself.)

Simple language (with repetition of 'and') emphasises the peace and simplicity of the action.

List of what must be done to love again: sentences begin with commands, e.g. 'take', 'peel'.

Emphasises joy from the start. Commas make you pause, to highlight the feeling.

Simple pleasure shown by one-word sentence.

Wine and bread have religious (Christian) meaning.

Repetition of 'heart' – appropriate in a love poem.

Love After Love

The time will come
When, with elation,
You will greet yourself arriving
At your own door, in your own mirror,
And each will smile at the other's welcome,

And say sit here. Eat.
You will love again the stranger who was your self.
Give wine. Give bread. Give back your heart
To itself, to the stranger who has loved you

All your life, whom you ignored
For another, who knows you by heart.
Take down the love-letters from the bookshelf

The photographs, the desperate notes,
Peel your own images from the mirror.
Sit. Feast on your life.

Sentences get shorter as the old complicated life becomes simpler.

Idea of celebrating, enjoying life again – 'Feast' refers back to wine and bread earlier.

Analysing the language use

- When you discuss the way the poet uses language:

  1 Make a **point**, e.g. The poet describes the slippers in detail.

  2 Refer to the **evidence**, e.g. 'embossed slippers, gold and black points curling'

  3 Comment on the **effect** of the language, e.g. The texture (embossed) and the colour show how unusual and special they are.

Top Tip!

Remember PEE:
- Point
- Evidence
- Effect

If you had to analyse the use of language in *Love After Love*, you could begin like this:

Grade C

Overall purpose of the poem given, to give context for the detailed comments that follow.

Language use identified (short sentence), and its purpose commented on.

> Walcott is writing a poem to show that coming to terms with ourselves and who we really are brings peace. From the beginning, he focuses on happiness – the strong word 'elation' makes this clear, and 'smile' and 'welcome' support it. He stresses that we are in our 'own' place and can enjoy the experience.
>
> He describes us returning to simple pleasures. 'Eat' is a one-word sentence, at the end of the line. This makes it important – perhaps Walcott is saying that we can feed ourselves, we do not need others. The mention of wine and bread, with their religious significance, makes the eating almost religious. Later in the poem this image of feasting is used again ('Feast on your life'). He is saying that we have enough memories and knowledge to feed us as long as we live.

Examples given to support purpose given. Brief reference to text.

Language use identified (image of feasting), and its effect and purpose commented on. Brief reference to the text.

Comparing language use

- When you compare two poems, part of your answer is likely to compare the way the poets use language.

Look at how language is used in these two extracts. The overall mood of the poems is very different – how does the language help to convey that mood?

'I' used a lot for emphasis

Words suggest hatching.

Sentence runs on over the ends of the lines – suggests movement.

Words suggest upward movement.

also movement from dark to light

> This room is breaking out
> of itself, cracking through
> its own walls
> in search of space, light,
> empty air.
> The bed is lifting out of
> its nightmares.
> From dark corners, chairs
> are rising up to crash through clouds.
>
> *This Room* by Imtiaz Dharker

list

sound effects

> I tried each satin-silken top –
>   was alien in the sitting-room.
> I could never be as lovely
>   as those clothes –
>   I longed
> for denim and corduroy.
>   My costume clung to me
>   and I was aflame,
> I couldn't rise up out of its fire,
>   half-English,
>   unlike Aunt Jamila.
>
> *Presents from my Aunts in Pakistan*
>   by Moniza Alvi

Alliteration emphasises the quality of the top.

Powerful word – shows feelings of speaker.

Simile – she compares herself to the clothes.

Alliteration emphasises the suffocation.

Metaphor – she is being burnt up.

Suggests image of the phoenix – but she can't be reborn (as the phoenix was).

Task

Compare the use of language in *This Room* and *Presents from my Aunts in Pakistan*. Include some of the points given above.

Comparing two poems

Key points

- Paper 2 Section A will ask you to **compare two poems**.

- The question will highlight **what aspects** of the poems you need to compare. This comparison must be the focus of your answer.

- Begin with a brief **introduction** and sum up with a **conclusion**.

- Support your views with **clear references** to the poems.

Reading the question

One poem is always named; you choose the poem to compare it with.

Compare *Nothing's Changed* with another poem from a different culture or tradition. Show how the people in the poems react to their surroundings. You should write about:
- the ideas in the poems
- the poets' attitudes to the situations they describe
- how the poets use language to show you these things.

Focus your comparison on this point. Don't compare the two poems in general terms.

The bullet points outline what you should write about.

Planning your answer

- When you have chosen which question to answer, and which poem you are going to compare with the named poem, spend five minutes planning your answer.

- Jot down ideas about each poem in turn. Use the bullet points in the question to organise these ideas. For example:

Island Man

<u>ideas</u>

seems at home at first
gradually he comes back to reality - London
he can imagine a better life but
he accepts his situation

<u>poet's attitude</u>

she stresses wonder of life in Caribbean
seems torn between two worlds - accepts both?
last line suggests being in London is a drag

<u>language</u>

sound effects - suggests waves of sea
vivid setting and detail
'groggily groggily' - doesn't want to wake
'heaves' - unwilling

Top Tip!

When you choose the second poem, make sure it will let you make good comparisons in the areas outlined in the question. (In the answers on pages 44–45, the student has chosen to compare *Nothing's Changed* with *Island Man*.)

Top Tip!

The bullet points in the question are very useful. They show you exactly what you should write about.
- Use them to brainstorm ideas when you plan your answer.
- Use them to structure your answer, by writing a paragraph on each bullet point.

Referring to the poems

- Make sure that you refer to **both poems** in your answer.

- Refer to **relevant details**. Keep the focus of the question in mind.

- You should **compare the texts**. Don't just write about one, then the other, without saying how they are similar or different.

- When referring to the texts, **link one text to the other**. Words and phrases such as 'however', 'similarly', 'in contrast', 'on the other hand' are useful when you do this.

Page 24

Using quotations and examples

- Always support your ideas by referring to the poems. There are different ways of doing this:

  - Refer to the poem **without quoting directly**:

  > Agard goes on to consider whether music is half-caste as well. He refers to the composer Tchaikovsky mixing black and white keys on the piano – which of course he had to do to produce a symphony.

  - **Include brief quotations** from the poem. Quote the exact words and put them inside inverted commas:

  > Tom Leonard's words are spelt as they are spoken by someone with a strong Scottish accent, for example 'wanna you scruff' and 'yi canny talk right'.

  - If you are **referring to a longer passage**, or you are quoting two or more lines of the poem, set the passage out on a new line, after a colon:

  > The language used to describe water cleverly portrays the sound of the water:
  > 'Imagine the drip of it,
  > the small splash, echo
  > in a tin mug'

Top Tip!

Don't waste time by copying out long quotations. When you are commenting on longer passages, it's better to write about them than to copy out chunks of text.

Comparing two poems

Writing the introduction

- Begin your answer with a brief introduction (one paragraph).
- Introduce both poems and relate them to the subject of the question.

You could write an **opening paragraph** to the question on page 42 like this:

First poem summarised briefly.

Further detail refers to the focus of the question (how the man reacts to the situation).

Grade C

Further detail refers to the focus of the question (the situation in the poem).

Second poem summarised briefly, and a clear comparison made.

> In 'Nothing's Changed', we have a picture of South Africa after the end of apartheid. The poet is suggesting that life has not improved, and has produced a protest poem which shows the unfairness in that country. The situation in 'Island Man' is different, because Grace Nichols reveals how a Caribbean island man still thinks of his home, but has to get up and cope with existence in London where he has moved. He may not be happy, but has chosen this way of living.

Top Tip!

Make sure your opening paragraph:
- refers to both poems
- refers to the focus of the question
- is brief and clear.

Good Points

- The student **focuses on the question**.
- The poems are **summarised briefly**.
- From the start, the student **compares the poems**.

Writing the main part of the answer

- In the main part of your answer you should write a detailed comparison of the two poems. You could follow this plan:

  1 Write in detail about one poem, using the bullet points in the question to organise your paragraphs.

  2 Then write in detail about the other poem, again using the bullet points.

  3 When discussing the second poem, refer back to the first where appropriate to make your comparisons.

You could write a **detailed comparison**, as below:

(Note: in the following answer, the student has already written about *Nothing's Changed*. These paragraphs focus on the second poem, *Island Man*. Only the beginning of the detailed comparison is shown.)

Clear signal that the student is now turning to the second poem.

Backs up points by close reference to the text, and by giving comments on the passages quoted.

New paragraph for a new point, but focus is still on the second poem.

Grade C

When we examine 'Island Man', we see that his situation is similar in that he, too, can imagine a better life. In his case, though, it is a beautiful life he has known already. Details such as 'the sound of blue surf' and 'fishermen pushing out to sea' give a vivid picture of the sound and sights of the homeland he loves so much, brought out by the repeated 's' sounds, which suggest the sound of the sea.

Island Man seems to accept his situation ('he always comes back...'), even though reluctantly, as suggested by the miserable last line 'Another London day'. This contrasts with the first poem, which can see no hope for black people in South Africa and where the speaker feels like turning to violence.

Focus is on the 'better life' in the second poem, though a comparison is made with the first poem.

Cross-reference to the first poem to show comparison.

Writing the conclusion

- In a final paragraph, summarise the key points you have made.
- You could also make a comment on how successful you think the poems are.

You could write a **concluding paragraph** like this:

Sums up the first poem's message.

Sums up the second poem's viewpoint. The student gives an opinion about the poem's success ('very clear').

Grade C

The way people react to their surroundings, therefore, is treated very differently in each poem. Tatamkhulu Afrika thinks violence is the only answer: in the last stanza there is the image of a bomb smashing the glass. The last line, though, returns us to the start, because 'Nothing's changed' (which is the title of the poem). 'Island Man', however, seems resigned to his life, and leaves his dreams behind to start 'Another London day'. The contrast between his life as it was and his life as it is has been made very clear.

'Therefore' signals a summing up. Note the student still has the focus of the question in mind.

Task

Show how *Half-Caste* and one other poem from a different culture present the feelings of people who do not feel part of the society around them.
Write about:
- the problems the people have
- their feelings
- how successfully their feelings are shown.

Raising your grade

If you want to raise your grade to C or above, you need to show these skills.

Refer to the poems effectively

- Make a **point** and back it up by **referring to** or **quoting from** the text.

> The scavengers, compared to the couple in the car, are ugly. The description 'gargoyle Quasimodo' shows this clearly by referring to two ugly images. ✔

- Choose **brief** quotations, and make sure they are **relevant** to the point you are making.
- Add a **comment** which explains why you are quoting from the text.
- Quote the words **exactly**, using **inverted commas** or **summarise** the text.

Make clear cross-references between poems

- Make sure you mention both poems in your **introduction**. Sum up their similarities and differences in your **conclusion**.
- When you discuss the second poem, **compare** it with the first whenever you can.
- Use words like '**whereas** in the first poem …' and 'in this poem, **however**, …' to show how you are comparing the poems.

> The lines are not divided into stanzas, so we seem to just follow her thoughts, whereas the second poem is much more organised, which shows … ✔

Show you are aware of the poets' techniques and purposes

- Don't just make comments on the effects of certain words or images. Go further and show that you are spotting a **deliberate technique** by the poet:

> The 'ice white glass, linen falls, single rose' is made to appear fragile and beautiful, which is <u>deliberately contrasted</u> with the world of the working blacks: 'wipe your fingers …' ✔

- Show in your comments that **you know why** the poet is using language in this way.

> The Gujerati script shows the problems of dealing with a foreign tongue. ✘

> The Gujerati script, even when translated, is alien to us. The poet is showing us how difficult it must be for the speaker to cope with two languages. ✔

Show you understand the poets' feelings, attitudes and ideas

- Don't just focus on the content. Discuss the **deeper meaning** and the **poets' attitude** to what they are describing. **Develop your comments** to show you really understand.

> The society we see in Two Scavengers is one that is in two parts. ✘

> The society we see in Two Scavengers is one that is in two parts. On one side there are the scavengers, and on the other … ✔

Read the question and an extract from the student's answer below.
This is only a practice task, but the notes show how it demonstrates Grade C qualities.

> Compare how language has been used in the endings of *This Room* and *Presents from my Aunts in Pakistan*.

This Room

Pots and pans bang together
In celebration, clang
Past the crowd of garlic, onions, spices,
Fly by the ceiling fan.
No one is looking for the door.

In all this excitement
I'm wondering where
I've left my feet, and why

My hands are outside, clapping.

Presents from my Aunts in Pakistan

Sometimes I saw Lahore –
          my aunts in shaded rooms,
screened from male visitors,
    sorting presents,
        wrapping them in tissue.

Or there were beggars, sweeper-girls
    and I was there –
        of no fixed nationality,
staring through fretwork
        at the Shalimar Gardens.

Grade C

Effective reference to the poem: brief and relevant to the point being made.

Shows awareness of the poet's purpose.

Now discusses the second poem, but makes comparisons with the first poem.

Shows awareness of the poet's technique, and adds a comment on the quotation.

Understands what the poet is feeling, backed up by evidence from the poem.

Shows awareness of the poet's technique (symbol).

The extract from 'This Room' begins with a lot of noise - lots of 'p's and the sound of 'pans bang', followed by the rhyme 'clang'. There is even a 'crowd of garlic, onions, spices', an image which makes them sound like spectators somewhere. This list stretches through the first sentence of the stanza, and it could make you think this is frightening as it builds up, but the final sentence takes the worry away:

'No one is looking for the door.'

Dharker feels as if everything is suddenly out of her control, and the way the sentences run over the lines in the second stanza back this up. Though the final line, ending with 'clapping', shows that she is excited about it.

'Presents from my Aunts in Pakistan' is much calmer. It begins with a rhyme, 'saw Lahore', which seems slow. The description of her aunts' existence is not full of movement like 'This Room.' Instead words like 'shaded' and 'screened' describe how they are hidden quietly away. This world seems safer, but lacks the 'excitement' of Dharker's room.

Alvi ends by describing herself as 'of no fixed nationality'. She is outside society. This is symbolised by the picture of her staring through the fretwork of the gates ...

Paper 1 Section B and Paper 2 Section B: Writing

Key points

- Section B of both English papers tests your writing skills.

- In each paper you have to choose just one question.

- In Paper 1 you have to write to argue, persuade and/or advise. In Paper 2 you have to inform, explain and/or describe.

Pages 62–85

- Section B of Paper 1 counts for 15% of your total mark. Section B of Paper 2 counts for a further 15% of your total mark.

- You should spend about 45 minutes on each answer. That means writing between one and two sides of paper.

The exam paper

This is an example of Paper 1 Section B. Paper 2 Section B is organised in exactly the same way.

Each paper consists of two sections. Section A (not given here) is the Reading questions.

In Paper 1 Section B (here) you have to write to argue, persuade, advise. In Paper 2 Section B (not given here) you have to write to inform, explain, describe.

Paper 1 Section B: Foundation Tier

WRITING TO ARGUE, PERSUADE OR ADVISE

Answer **one** question.

You are advised to spend about 45 minutes on this section.

EITHER

3 Write an article for your local newspaper, **arguing** that there is too much pressure on teenagers and that they should be allowed to enjoy 'the best years of their lives'.

You might wish to write about:

- pressures at school
- pressures at home
- why being a teenager should be a happy time.

Remember to:

- write an article
- choose the right language to argue.   *(27 marks)*

Choose one question only in Section B.

OR

4 Writing as a celebrity chef, produce a newspaper column to **persuade** parents to encourage their children to eat healthily.

You might wish to write about:

- why healthy eating is important
- what children should eat
- how parents can encourage children to eat healthily.

Remember to:

- write a persuasive newspaper column
- use the right language for parents
- focus on healthy eating.   *(27 marks)*

Use the bullet points to help you plan your answer.

The skills you will be tested on

The questions in Section B of each paper are designed to test your writing skills. This table outlines the skills that are tested, and explains what you have to do to get good marks.

The skill you need to show	How to get good marks

1 Communicate clearly and imaginatively

Pages 50–51 and 62–85

- Think of ideas that are **relevant** to the question, and present them **clearly**.
- Make your answer **varied** and **imaginative** so that it keeps the reader's interest.

2 Write for different readers and purposes

Pages 50–51 and 62–85

- You must know how to write for a specific **purpose** (e.g. to advise) and how to write in a specific **form** (e.g. a letter).
- You also need to know how to target a specific **audience** (e.g. younger people).

3 Organise your ideas

Pages 52–53

- Give your ideas some kind of **structure**.
- Write a good **opening**, a clear **sequence of paragraphs** for the main section and a powerful **conclusion**.
- Write in **paragraphs** and **vary the length** of the paragraphs for effect.

4 Write in sentences

Pages 54–55

- Your writing must **make sense**.
- Make sure your sentences are **varied and effective** and that they suit the type of writing.
- Write sentences of **different lengths**.
- Write sentences of **different types** (e.g. questions, commands, statements).

5 Use a wide vocabulary

Pages 56–57

- Use words that suit the **purpose** and **audience** of your writing.
- Try to use **interesting** and **powerful** words.
- **Vary** your words and avoid repetition.
- Use **techniques** such as imagery, repetition and contrasts, where they suit the type of writing.

6 Punctuate your sentences accurately

Pages 58–59

- Make sure each sentence begins with a **capital letter** and ends with a **full stop**.
- Use a **wider range** of punctuation where you can, such as commas, apostrophes, exclamation marks, question marks and quotation marks.

7 Spell accurately

Pages 60–61

- You need to know how to **spell words you use regularly**.
- Apply **spelling rules** whenever possible.
- You will gain more marks if you can spell a wider range of words.

Ideas and planning

Key points

- You should spend **up to 10 minutes planning** your answer.

- First, **think of ideas** that you can use in your writing.

- When doing this, you should always keep in mind the **purpose** and **audience** of the task.

- Then **structure** your ideas and **develop** them.

Thinking of ideas: audience and purpose

- First, highlight the **key words** in the question title. These will help you identify the purpose and audience of the task.

- The **purpose** of your response will be to argue, persuade, advise, inform, explain or describe.

- The **audience** (the people you are writing for) may be of a certain age or from a certain background, e.g. children or school governors.

- The audience and purpose affect the **style** and **tone** of your writing (e.g. informal or formal, serious or funny), the **form** of your writing (e.g. a letter, speech or article), and its **content**.

This is how you could make notes on a question from Paper 1:

purpose: formal writing

Write a **section for a school booklet** to be sent to **teachers** applying for a job at your school. Offer them **advice** on how to **cope with any problems** they might encounter.

audience: will need clear but basic advice, since they will be just starting the job

purpose: to identify the problems and tell the new teachers exactly how they might cope with them

This is how you could make notes on a question from Paper 2:

purpose: explain, don't just inform

purpose: focus on activities away from school/work

Explain why **you spend your free time in the way you do**. Write about:
- the way you spend your **evenings**
- what you do at **weekends**
- **why you find these activities interesting and worthwhile**.

purpose: to give the reasons why you spend your time in these ways

Top Tip!

The questions in Paper 2 often don't say exactly who the audience is. If that happens, assume that you are writing for the examiner. Your style should be quite formal.

Structuring your ideas

- Put your ideas together, first of all as **brief notes**.

- You could produce your ideas as a **spider diagram**:

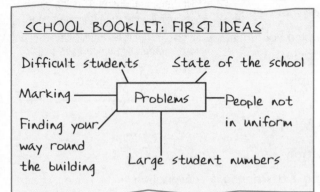

- Or you could **list them** in the order you might deal with them in your actual answer:

Free time
Evenings – homework, Tai Kwon Do, music,
X Box

Weekends – town, football matches,
cleaning (!), friends

Why – relaxation, fitness, self-improvement,
a change

Developing your ideas

- Now develop the basic ideas by adding **further detail** on your plan.

- Although planning time is short, you will benefit later. It will be easier to write the actual answer, because you will know **exactly what details to mention** in each section.

You could begin to **develop the ideas** for the school booklet like this.

School booklet

Difficult students:
Problems: aggressive to teachers –
regular fights – lots of exclusions
Advice: try listening and being
understanding; don't be too strict but
apply the rules

State of the school:
Problems: needs repairs – old desks –
leaking roof – vandalism
Advice: set an example by keeping your
classroom tidy/get any graffiti removed
that you see; set up after-school
litter patrols

Here's another example. The writing task is:
'Describe the person you most admire in the world.'

1 Uncle Frank: age, kind of person he is, how others see him, why he's my hero – story to explain this
2 How he found out about his illness. The effect it had: job/home.
3 Aunty Jane's situation. What she said. What they did. The outcome. Family involvement.
4 What he's been like since, with other people and on trips to the hospital.
5 Fundraising: his pain and his gains, reports in local paper, award from Queen
6 His future plans: ending with hope, quote from Uncle

Good Points

- The notes are broken into sections. These could also show where you begin a new paragraph. Sometimes, you might want to turn one of the sections into two or three shorter paragraphs.
- There is a 'core idea' for each section, then further detail on what could be included.

Task

1 Identify the key words in the question on the right.

2 Do a spider diagram or make notes on some ideas that you could use to answer the question.

Write a speech to give to your year group, informing them about what the school offers out of lesson time. You might wish to mention:
- sports teams
- clubs and societies
- trips.

Structure and paragraphs

Key points

- You will be awarded marks for how well you **structure** your writing.

- That means writing an effective **introduction**, developing your ideas in the **main section**, then ending with a powerful **conclusion**.

- It also means **organising and linking your paragraphs**.

Top Tip!

The time you spend planning your answer is very important. Put your ideas in a logical order, then write a paragraph or two on each main idea.

Pages 50–51

The introduction

- Your first paragraph should **grab the reader's attention**.

- There are **many effective ways** you could do this, e.g. a description, a conversation, a moment of high drama, an anecdote (a story about someone or something).

If your task was 'Describe the person you most admire in the world', you could begin like this:

Opening sentence is relevant – gives an immediate sense of someone you admire.

> Even our mayor admires my Uncle Frank, and gave a dinner in his honour last year. He said: ' What Frank has done is show just how much a person can achieve when they set their mind to it. He has overcome a lot of disadvantages. He's also worked tirelessly for others, even though most people in his position might expect others to look after them. Everyone in this town agrees that he is a great man.'

Quotation makes Frank seem real, and brings the writing to life.

The mayor's speech sets out Frank's qualities and his situation. It shows how much Frank is admired by everyone.

The conclusion

- Your final paragraph should **round off** your piece of writing.

- It should leave the reader with a **good impression**.

- If you can, **link the conclusion with the introduction**.

- Here is a possible ending to the piece of writing on Uncle Frank.

> ' I'm not great, like that mayor said,' Uncle Frank once told me laughing. ' It was kind of him, but I'm just a stubborn man who does what he thinks is right. I've always lived like that, and I always will. I won't give in, but that's not special, it's just the way I am.' But he is special, of course, and that is why I admire him so much.

Good Points ✓

- The student sums up Uncle Frank's character in this anecdote.
- The final sentence links directly to the title.
- The ending refers back to the opening paragraph (the mayor's speech).

Organising and linking paragraphs

- Begin each paragraph with a **topic sentence**. This states the main idea of the paragraph.

- The remaining sentences then develop the idea in more detail, e.g.

The government has its priorities wrong … — you then say why, or what the priorities should be

There are three steps to perfect happiness … — which you then name and discuss

Please attend to these safety requirements … — you then list the safety requirements.

- Link your paragraphs with **connectives** – words or phrases that show the reader you are **linking ideas**. For example:

  - chronological (time sequence), e.g. *At first, Then, Later*

  - logical order, e.g. *Therefore, Consequently, As a result*

  - contrast, e.g. *On the other hand, In contrast*

  - a simple ordering of ideas, e.g. *Firstly, Secondly, Finally*

  - a development of ideas, e.g. *Because of this, What is more, In addition*

Top Tip!

You will gain marks if you vary the length of your paragraphs for effect. A short paragraph, for example, will stand out from the rest.

Look at how this student organises and links her paragraphs in a piece about an eventful holiday:

Grade C

Topic sentence introduces feelings about holidays.

chronological link word

topic sentence

Connective links to previous paragraph.

> My holidays used to be boring. I spent my mornings pretending to do the jobs my mother left me before she went to work, and each afternoon I just watched the TV. In the evenings, I just looked out of the window, wishing that something would happen. It even seemed crazy to me at the time, but I wished school would start again so that I could be back with friends. I was even glad that I had a goldfish to talk to. I looked forward to taking my tortoise for walks round the garden.
>
> Then I met Garth, and my life was totally changed. He smiled over the hedge and that was that - he was my new neighbour and he was perfect.
>
> Suddenly, life was better. It was no longer a matter of being bored, it was all about trying to find enough time to get ready and to be with Garth. It was about looking my best and looking out for Garth …

Long opening paragraph with lists of boring activities – shows the mood of the writer.

Short paragraph for effect: contrasts to what went before and suggests life and change.

Short topic sentence introduces more lively ideas.

Another list, but this time it contrasts with first paragraph: items are shorter, suggesting more life and action.

Task

Find an article at least three paragraphs long in a magazine. Identify the topic sentences and the link words and phrases. Notice how they help you follow the stages of the article. (Noticing how other people write can help you to improve your own writing.)

Sentences

Key points

- Use a **range of sentence length**: short, medium and long.
- Use a **range of sentence types**: statements, questions, commands and exclamations.
- Include **subordinate clauses**, e.g. 'so that …', 'until …'
- Make sure the **style** and **tone** of your sentences suit the **purpose** and **audience** of the task.

Short sentences

- Short sentences can produce a **feeling of simplicity**, but that does not mean they cannot be powerful. For example, this moving incident from Ernest Hemingway's *A Farewell to Arms* is mostly made up of short sentences:

> Mrs Henry has had a haemorrhage   The doctor is with her.
>   Is it dangerous?
>   It is very dangerous.   The nurse went into the room and shut the door. I sat outside in the hall. Everything was gone inside of me. I did not think. I could not think. I knew she was going to die

- Short sentences can rush, one after the other, to provide **excitement**:

  He began to run. The man followed. His heart was racing.
  The man was catching him. He had no choice. He dived into the icy water.

- A short sentence after a series of longer sentences can make a **quick but powerful point**:

  The situation right across the country is one that leads many to despair. Hospitals struggling with under-funding and short of both staff and resources are trying to keep our aging population on its feet whilst billions are being wasted on defence contracts and over-spending. It makes me angry.

- A **single word sentence** can create a particular effect, but don't use this technique too much.

  We waited for more information from the governors. Nothing. What a waste of time!

Longer sentences

You can **join two short sentences** together by using 'and', 'so' or 'but':

The Prime Minister has not told the truth. He must resign.

The Prime Minister has not told the truth **and** he must resign.

The Prime Minister has told the truth **but** he must resign.

- **Longer sentences** often include a subordinate clause, which would not make sense on its own:

  Because the Prime Minister has not told the truth, he must resign.

  The Prime Minister must resign, if he has any sense of honour.

  Although the Prime Minister has resigned, nothing has really changed.

  The Prime Minister has resigned, which is a tragedy.

Top Tip!

If you mix different lengths and types of sentence you will gain marks. In particular, including subordinate clauses makes your sentences much more interesting.

Creating effects

- Longer and more complex sentences are useful for **explaining ideas**:

  We cannot overlook the effect on the local wildlife and the countryside, which are bound to suffer. On the other hand, we know how poor the local people are and they must have a say in their own future.

- They provide **more detail** in descriptive writing:

  I see the old lady every summer, sitting at the bottom of the steps with her wise eyes and wide smile, and she seems unchanged by the years.

Here is an extract from a piece of descriptive writing:

These two long sentences set the scene and create an impression of time passing slowly.

> At dawn, the sky was grey and there was the sound of crows in the woods behind the house. There was no traffic, just the animals in the fields and the lightest of breezes, rattling the window at times. Then the children were about. The boards started to creak. There were loud voices down the hall.

Grade C

These three short sentences show action – the house is waking up.

Questions, commands and exclamations

- **Rhetorical questions** do not expect an answer. Instead, they are a way of making a powerful statement:

  Do you know any school that has all the facilities it really needs?

  – This really means: 'There are no schools that have all the facilities they need.'

  Is it ever acceptable to value animals more than humans?

  – This really means: 'It is never acceptable to value animals more than humans.'

- **Commands** are a way of addressing the reader directly:

  Buy this book and your life will change overnight.

- **Exclamations** show emotional reactions and aim to make the reader react the same way:

  What a disgrace!

  The results were stunning!

Top Tip!

Different effects suit different purposes and audiences.
For example, rhetorical questions are useful when writing to argue or persuade.

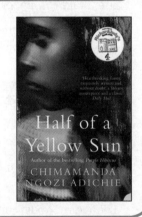

Task

This is an extract from a leaflet about a theme park. Rewrite it so that the sentences are more varied and interesting. You can alter the order and add extra words if you need to.

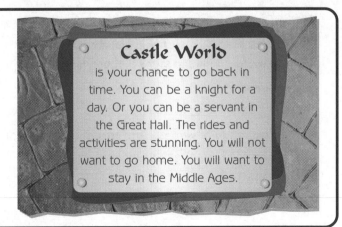

Castle World

is your chance to go back in time. You can be a knight for a day. Or you can be a servant in the Great Hall. The rides and activities are stunning. You will not want to go home. You will want to stay in the Middle Ages.

Vocabulary

Key points

- A wide vocabulary helps your writing in many ways, e.g.
  - You can use the **appropriate** word for the **purpose** or **audience**.
  - It means you **avoid repeating** words.
  - It makes your writing **more interesting**.
  - It means you can be **more precise** about the meaning or the effect.
- Use **imagery** to gain higher marks.

Using appropriate words

- Choose words to suit the **purpose** and **audience** of your writing:
  - If you are writing a letter to inform your school or college governors about problems, the language should be **formal**:

  It is with sadness that I have to bring this serious matter to your attention …

  - On the other hand, a letter describing problems to a friend would be **informal**:

  You'll never guess what happened to me. It was some big deal at the time …

  - **Emotive words** (words which persuade the reader to feel something strongly) are useful in persuasive writing, e.g. *broken-hearted, abandoned*.

  - **Technical words** are useful in information writing, e.g. *species, habitat* (for the natural world); *secondary, vocational* (for education).

Avoiding repetition

- In your letter to the governors, for example, instead of repeating 'serious', you might use 'grave' or 'important'.
- The letter to your friend might use a range of different words to describe something bad, e.g. *terrible, awful, tragic, criminal, drastic, mind-numbing*.

Using more interesting words

- Adjectives and adverbs can make your sentences more interesting, e.g.

  The book describes a search, but it is the characters that capture our attention.

  The book describes a <u>mysterious</u> quest, but it is the <u>beautifully-drawn</u> characters that engage our attention.

- Longer, more difficult words are often impressive, e.g. *an <u>atrocious</u> attack, an <u>unacceptable</u> request.*

Using more precise words

- Try to avoid nouns and verbs that are very general, e.g.

  She <u>ran</u> to the <u>shops</u>.

  She <u>jogged all the way</u> to the <u>newsagent's on the corner</u>.

- The exact noun or verb you use creates a **particular effect**, e.g.

  Maria <u>lounged</u> in the <u>conservatory</u>.

  The dog <u>whimpered</u> in the <u>shed</u>.

Top Tip!

Remember to use words and phrases to connect paragraphs and ideas, e.g. 'First', 'Therefore', 'Because of this', 'Yet'.

Page 53

Using imagery

- **Similes** make a comparison using 'like' or 'as':

  Although your father seems <u>as old-fashioned as a sideboard</u>, in this case he is right ...

  Your opportunity to work for that company might seem <u>like a ticket to paradise</u> right now, but ...

- **Metaphors** state things that are not really true, but the comparison has a strong effect:

  Even though <u>your teachers come from the age of the dinosaurs</u>, they can teach you many things ...

  <u>You exploded</u> when I last suggested this, but, <u>at the risk of causing another world war</u>, I must tell you again that ...

> ### Top Tip!
> When you are checking through your work, don't be afraid to cross words out and replace them with better ones. You will gain marks for using a higher level word, even if it is spelt incorrectly.

'Even though your teachers come from the age of the dinosaurs ...'

Notice how this C grade student uses a wide vocabulary, with imagery:

'my existence' avoids repetition of 'my life'	precise and powerful verb
simile	
powerful metaphor	linking word
	powerful adjective

> My life in the hospital kitchen is very different from my existence at school. I slave over sinks of boiling water. There are cooking pots to scrub and I am like a robot: wash the pan, leave it to drain, and move on to the next. Although in school I am with my friends, in my night-time hell I am generally alone. There is just the extreme heat, the sweat from my brow and the clashing of pans for hours on end.

Task

This is an extract from a student's description of his uncle. Rewrite it to:
- use more interesting and precise words
- avoid repetition (e.g. 'spends a lot of time').

Can you include some imagery?

> At home, Uncle Tom spends a lot of time in his study. That's not because he likes marking school work ... it's to get away from Aunt Sylvia. He spends a lot of time in school as well, which is 3 miles down the road.

Punctuation

Page 55

Key points

- You need to use **basic punctuation**, such as full stops and capital letters.
- To obtain higher marks, you need to use a **range of punctuation**.
- You should **aim to use** commas, apostrophes, question marks and exclamation marks, speech marks, brackets and dashes. If you can use colons and semi-colons, even better.

Commas

- Use commas to:

  1 separate the **items in a list**:

  We have a first class <u>health service, education system and defence force</u>.

  Note that the final item before 'and' (*education system*) does not need a comma after it.

  2 separate **clauses** from the main part of a sentence:

  <u>Although we sometimes doubt politicians</u>, they are working to make our lives better, <u>so we should respect them</u>.

  3 separate a **phrase** that gives extra information about something:

  The Prime Minister, <u>a man of great wisdom</u>, is supported by his ministers.

  4 separate **connectives** that begin sentences:

  Finally, However, Two days later, After all, etc.

Apostrophes

- Apostrophes are used to:

  1 show **possession**:

  – If the 'owner' is singular, the apostrophe goes before the 's', e.g.

  Europe's problems, my aunt's car

  – If the 'owner' is plural, the apostrophe goes after the 's', e.g.

  schools' problems, footballers' wives

  2 show where a letter or letters have been removed (an **omission**), e.g.

  Is not it? ➝ *Isn't it?*; *You are losing* ➝ *You're losin'*

Top Tip!

Remember that *its* is used to show ownership (like 'his' or 'hers'), e.g. *She pulled its tail.*
It's (with an apostrophe) stands for 'it is', e.g. *It's raining.*

Question marks and exclamation marks

- Remember to use a **question mark** at the end of every question.
- Don't use too many **exclamation marks**. They should only be used to show humour, or strong or sudden feelings like anger, surprise or delight.

In this extract, a doctor explains how he struggles with difficult patients:

Question mark makes it clear how he said the sentence.

> You have to be firm with them. On one occasion, <u>an old lady</u> complained so much that I could stand it no longer. 'Problems?' I said. 'You think you have <u>problems</u>? You should try doing my job!'

Comma separates the phrase adding information to the main clause.

Emotion is shown by exclamation mark.

Speech marks

Follow these guidelines:

Put speech marks round the words that are spoken, including any punctuation (here a question mark).

You can even put the speaker in the middle of a spoken sentence, for variety.

'Are you well?' asked my mother.

'He looks strange,' said my father.

I replied, 'I'm as well as could be expected, under the circumstances.'

'In that case,' said my mother, 'we can proceed.'

'But I don't want to go to the dentist,' I said. 'Can't it wait until next week?'

If someone speaks more than one sentence but the speaker is mentioned in between, use a full stop and capital letter, like this.

When the speech is not a question or exclamation, put a comma at the end of it.

If the speaker comes first, add a comma then the speech in speech marks. Begin the speech with a capital letter, and end with a full stop.

Top Tip!

Although you are unlikely to be writing a story in your exam, you might want to include some speech in your response, so you need to know how to punctuate it correctly.

Adding information

• **Brackets** can be used to give extra information, e.g.

His hands lost no speed, his hands looked as fast as Ali's (except when he got hit) and his face was developing a murderous appetite.

The Fight by Norman Mailer

• A **colon** (:) can introduce a list, following a general statement:

This town can be proud of its heritage: the cathedral, the castle and its famous men and women who fought for what was right.

• A **colon** can also introduce a clause that leads on from or explains the first clause:

She was terrified: the exam was only three hours away.

• A **semi-colon** links two clauses that are equally important:

Tammy likes swimming; Katie prefers sailing.

• **Dashes** can be used in the same way.

• Dashes can also **make information stand out**, e.g.

Billionaire Chelsea owner Roman Abramovich has bought himself a new toy – a £72 million yacht.

The Russian oil tycoon – worth £3.5 billion – stunned onlookers when the 378ft craft put into the South of France last night. *The Sun*

Top Tip!

1 When you write a dash, make sure you include a space before and after it. Otherwise it looks like a hyphen.

2 Don't use dashes too much, as it can look as if you are just adding text thoughtlessly.

Task

1 Add the punctuation to this sentence:
jakes guitar teacher rang he said hes going to a gig in birmingham

2 Correct the punctuation in this sentence:
'Its hopeless is'nt it!' she sighed. all the sock's are muddled up

Spelling and accuracy

Key points

- To gain a grade C, you need to spell a wide range of words **accurately**.
- Follow the **spelling rules**, and use **strategies** to master the spelling of difficult words. Most of this should be familiar from Key Stage 3, but it is always good to remind yourself of the rules and strategies.

Spelling rules: plurals

- Add -s to make the plural of a word, e.g. *house → houses, pool → pools*

Exceptions:

- Words ending in -ss, -sh, -ch, -x: add -es, e.g. *glasses, bushes, matches, foxes*
- Words ending in consonant + y: change -y to -ies, e.g. *lady → ladies, try → tries*
- Words ending in -f: you usually change -f to -ves, e.g. *loaf → loaves, leaf → leaves*
- Some words ending in -o: add -es, e.g. *tomatoes, potatoes*
- Some words don't follow these rules, e.g. *children, women, mice, sheep*

Spelling rules: verbs

- Add -ing or -ed to make different parts of the verb, e.g.

  form → forming → formed, watch → watching → watched

Exceptions:

- Short verbs ending in vowel + consonant: double the consonant, e.g.

  drop → dropping → dropped, fit → fitting → fitted

- Longer verbs ending in vowel + consonant: double the consonant only if the emphasis is on the final syllable, e.g.

  admit → admitting, prefer → preferring, BUT *benefit → benefiting*

- Verbs ending in -e: drop the -e, e.g.

  decide → deciding → decided, state → stating → stated

- Many common verbs are irregular in the past tense, e.g.

  fight → fought, begin → began, meet → met

Spelling rules: prefixes and suffixes

- **Prefixes** are letters added at the start of a word to change its meaning:
  - in-, un-, im-, ir-, mis- and dis- often form opposites, e.g. *invisible, unfair, impossible, mistrust*
  - pre- and fore- mean 'in front', 'before', e.g. *prefer, foreground*.
  - Other prefixes include ex- and re- (again), e.g. *export, return*.
- **Suffixes** are letters added at the end of a word to change its meaning:
  - -able, -ible and -uble mean that something is possible, e.g. *legible, soluble*.
  - -ful means 'full of', e.g. *careful, peaceful* (NB not -full).
  - -less means 'without', e.g. *careless, endless*
  - -ation, -ition, -ution form a noun from a verb, e.g.

    create → creation, pollute → pollution

  - Drop a final -e before a suffix that begins with a vowel, e.g.

    invite + -ation = invitation, forgive + -able = forgivable

Spelling strategies

- The best way to master spelling is to look words up in a **dictionary** while you are writing. (You cannot use a dictionary in the exam.)

- Do **not** use **spell checker** programs. They don't tell you if a word is spelt correctly, only if it exists – and they make you a lazy speller.

- Compile a **list** of words you often misspell. Learn the correct spellings.

- **Learn** these words that are often misspelt.

all right	business	environment	occasionally
argument	coming	favourite	persuade
beautiful	definitely	friend	receive
beginning	develop	immediately	sense
believe	disappear	necessary	separate

Know the difference

- Some common words **sound the same** but are spelt differently. Learn these and look out for others:

  your (belonging to you) and you're (you are)

  their (belonging to them), they're (they are) and there (any other use)

  where (place), were (verb) and we're (we are)

  too (as well or very), two (the number) and to (any other use)

  whose (belonging to someone), who's (who is)

  quiet (calm), quite (a bit)

  accept (take), except (apart from)

  effect (noun), affect (verb)

Top Tip!

Don't be afraid to make alterations. However, although there are no marks for neatness, you must make sure the end result is legible, or you will lose marks.

Other spelling tips

- Use **mnemonics** (memory joggers), e.g.
  Remember there is *iron* in the *environment*, a *rat* in *separate*, *finite* in *definite* and a *cog* in *recognise*.

- Group words into **families**, where part of the word is the same, e.g.
  success, successful, succeed; *writing, writer, written*

- **Say the word** in your mind as it is spelt, e.g.
  Fe*bru*ary, Wed*nes*day

- **Chunking** – break words into smaller parts, e.g.
  ex-treme-ly, re-le-vant

Checking and correcting

- Spend five minutes at the end **checking** and **improving** your writing. This is important because vocabulary, punctuation and spelling **can all be improved**.

- **Read** through your response very slowly, as if reading aloud, and be prepared to **alter** your work whenever necessary.

Task

Check this writing and correct the spelling mistakes.

Why we should eat healthy food
People should except the argument that eating healthy food is good for us. It makes our weight disapear and has a good sychologicle affect on our state of mind. It doesnt matter if we ocasionaly have a cake or some choclate, but we should definately eat fruit and vegatables every day and losts of fruit; that's the only way to improof ourselfs and our society.

Writing to argue

Key points

- One of the questions in Section B of Paper 1 lets you **write to argue**.

- When you write to argue, you **present and develop a point of view** about something.

- Your answer should refer to the **other point of view**, be **well structured** and use **techniques** to convince the reader.

Presenting a point of view

- Your main task is to present your **point of view**. For example, it could be that students should wear school uniform, or that people should not eat meat.

- Make your point of view **clear from the start** of your answer.

- In your planning, jot down some ideas that **support** your point of view. Then note some **opposing** ideas. Think about how you would answer these points.

- Show that you are **aware of the opposite point of view** by referring to it in your answer.

In this extract, a student is arguing that there should be more money for schools.

> **Top Tip!**
>
> It helps if you believe in the point of view that you are arguing for. However, if you don't have a personal view on the issue, it doesn't matter. Choose one side of the argument and pretend that you are passionate about it!

Writer's own view is clear from the start.

The opposite viewpoint is referred to very briefly, but immediately attacked (note: 'But').

Grade C

We all know that more money is needed for schools. The extra books and equipment it can buy help them improve. We can see this because independent schools charge fees and use them to buy all the latest books and technology, and they have a good reputation.

Yes, the government points out that the quality of teaching is the most important thing. But teaching must be better when every student has a book and does not have to share, or has a PC on which to access the internet. So funding is vital for schools.

Reason for view is explained, and an example given (independent schools).

Writer's own point of view is stated strongly again.

Good Points

- The student's view is clear from the start.
- There is a brief mention of the other side of the argument.
- The opposite viewpoint is immediately dismissed so that the writer's own point of view can be developed.

Structure

- When you write an argument, you should be as **clear and logical** as possible. Structure is important.

- Make sure the main points are covered in a **logical and sensible order**.

- Begin a **new paragraph** for each **new point**.

- Introduce each main point with a **topic sentence**. The other sentences should develop that point.

Page 53

- Use **connectives** to show the links between points, such as 'however', 'on the other hand'.

- Make an impact on the reader with your **introduction** and **conclusion**.

Introduction

- Your introduction (paragraph 1) should **present the topic** and **state your attitude** to it.

Compare these two introductions, which have been given different grades. The 'How To Improve' box tells you the main points to improve in order to move the Grade D response to a Grade C. The students are writing an article for an employers' magazine, to argue for or against work experience.

> When I was told about work experience I wondered whether I would like it, and it was quite a difficult thing to do but in the end I quite liked it. Some people say work experience is a waste of time, and I know what they mean because I felt that too. Though I suppose it helps students get to know what real life is like.

Grade D

How To Improve

- The student presents the topic of work experience, but it isn't clear what his or her point of view is. Is the argument for or against work experience?
- The student moves from work experience being difficult, to it being enjoyable, to it being useful – this is confusing for the reader.

Point of view is stated at start.

Opposite point of view is referred to, then dismissed.

> In my opinion, work experience is a good thing. Some people argue that it is a waste of time, but I am going to show that it helps students get to know what real life is like. There are many things in its favour ...

Grade C

Good Points

- The student's point of view is clear from the start.
- There is some reference to another point of view.
- The student shows how s/he is going to develop the argument (by discussing the things in favour of work experience).
- The style is formal, which suits the purpose and audience.

TYPES OF WRITING

Development

- The main part of your answer should **develop your main points** logically. You can do this by:
  - giving **reasons** for your opinion
  - going into your points in more **detail**
  - giving one or more **examples**
  - providing some **evidence** for your views, e.g. facts and figures, personal experience, quotations from other people.

Look at this plan, by a student who did his work experience in a garage.

> PLAN
> Introduction
> Para 2: what I learnt about working in a team
>   responsibilities/being supported
> Para 3: how I enjoyed the tasks
>   taking apart engines/breakdown outings
> Para 4: what I learnt that I would not have learnt at school
>   dealing with real problems/longer hours
> Para 5: what happened to my friends
>   bad bosses/boring work/unfriendly workmates
> Para 6: why it is a good experience
>   school is too protected/we will have to work
> Conclusion:
>   why it was so useful

main point

idea for developing the main point

Top Tip!

As part of the planning, jot down the main points of your arguments. Put them in a sensible order, then follow this plan to give a good structure to the main part of your answer.

Pages 50–51

Good Points

- The argument is developed logically:
  - what he got out of it
  - others' problems
  - why it is still valuable.
- Different viewpoints are included.
- Each main point is given a new paragraph.
- There is an introduction and conclusion.

Conclusion

- The **conclusion** should sum up your opinion.
- Try to write an ending which will **stick in the memory**. Don't just tail off ...

> So, when I looked back on the two weeks, I realised that the problems didn't mean I hadn't learnt a lot and enjoyed myself. It was great to be covered in oil and I even feel that I am now better prepared for a working life. I would recommend work experience to anyone!

Top Tip!

The conclusion is the last thing the examiner will read before giving you a mark, so make it as clear and lively as possible.

Grade C

Good Points

- The student makes it clear that he is summing up ('So, when I looked back ...').
- The main point of view is stated again.
- It is a personal response, not a general statement.
- The conclusion is positive and enthusiastic.

Using a range of techniques

- Use a variety of techniques to present your argument effectively:
  - **anecdotes**: telling a story about someone/something that backs up your point
  - **quotations**: quoting what experts say
  - **rhetorical questions**: questions that are really a strong way of stating your view
  - **direct address**: addressing the reader directly to make them think about the point you are making
  - **lists**: building up a list of facts or evidence to make your point strongly
  - **varying the length** of your sentences.

This extract from a letter to the local council includes many of these techniques. It argues that more needs to be done for local residents.

Grade C

rhetorical question

Dear Sir,

Does our city have to have graffiti and litter and loads of junk in the streets? You collect our taxes and say you are concerned about our problems, but nothing ever seems to improve. I am tired of living in slum conditions on my housing estate, and I know that you can do something about it. You need a positive drive to improve our quality of life.

We often receive your leaflets, telling us how our neighbourhoods are safer and cleaner and how new action schemes are making our lives better. But we do not believe it. When the mayor writes:

'We can celebrate, because studies show all the improvements in our lives'

we are simply amazed. He seems to have no idea of what it is really like.

If you ever bothered to visit us you would see the truth for yourself. Our bins are always overflowing. There are abandoned cars, which teenagers love torching. The walls of buildings are covered in graffiti ...

direct address

strong statement of the point of view

Topic sentence introduces opposite point of view.

Words of an 'expert' are quoted, then argued against.

Connective shows the reader that the view is going to be criticised.

effective short sentence to end paragraph

list of problems

Good Points

- The writer has made his or her point of view clear, and referred to another viewpoint.
- The letter has a clear and logical structure.
- It begins with a powerful introduction which states the point of view.
- It uses techniques such as rhetorical question, quotation and list.
- The reader is guided through the text by topic sentences and connectives.

Task

Write an article for a local newspaper, arguing that your town, village or city needs improvement.

- Give it a clear and logical structure.
- State your point of view, but refer to a different viewpoint as well.
- Include some techniques to make your readers agree with your argument.

Writing to persuade

Key points

- One of the questions in Section B of Paper 1 lets you **write to persuade**.

- When you write to persuade, you try to get the reader to **do something or believe something**.

- Your answer should be **well structured** and use **techniques** to convince the reader.

- It should have a **tone** that suits the **purpose** and the **audience** of the task.

Structuring ideas

- As part of the **planning**, jot down your main ideas.

- Put them in a **sensible order** so that one idea **flows logically** from another.

- Then develop your main points by adding **further ideas**.

- Follow your plan to give a good structure to your answer.

Look at this plan for a letter to persuade an elderly relative to protect herself against dangers in the home.

Pages 50–51

main point

idea for developing the main point

> PLAN
>
> Intro: the need to be secure
> she is an important part of the family
> Para 2: action needed to protect her against burglars
> needs modern locks, an alarm, etc.
> Para 3: other problems
> old gas cooker; bad wiring
> Para 4: the benefits which will come from greater protection
> she can be more relaxed; cheaper home insurance
> Conclusion:
> how everyone in the family will feel better knowing she
> is safe

her need
↓
problems
↓
benefits from taking action

Top Tip!

There are different ways of persuading people. You might want to persuade readers by presenting a logical argument. In that way, persuasion can be like writing to argue.

When you persuade, however, you don't have to include more than one point of view.

For example, you might be writing a letter to persuade an elderly relative to protect herself against dangers in the home (as in the plan below). All you need to do is stress the need for more protection. You don't have to wonder if she may already be well protected.

Good Points

- The plan sets out ideas in a sensible order. It lists the current problems and then moves on to the benefits which would come from taking action.
- The main points are given (underlined), then developed by giving detail and examples.
- The introduction stresses the dangers but the conclusion stresses the benefits, so the persuasion has a clear direction.

Emotive language

- **Emotive language** is language which makes the reader feel something. It is a very effective technique when writing to persuade.

This is part of Nelson Mandela's speech when he was sworn in as the first black president of South Africa. Note the emotive language (in purple). Think about what the president wants to make the audience feel.

> We dedicate this day to the heroes and heroines in this country and the rest of the world who sacrificed in many ways and surrendered their lives so that we could be free. Their dreams have become reality. Freedom is their reward.

Compare these two opening paragraphs to persuade Grandma to make herself more secure. They have been awarded different grades:

> You are not safe in your home! I'm really worried that someone could break in or that you could be harmed by a fire! Your gas fires and cooker have not been checked recently! Why not!! Just follow my suggestions, and you'll be alright.

Grade D

How To Improve

- The student addresses Grandma, but the language is general. It needs some emotive language to make the reader feel something. All the feeling at the moment is coming from the exclamation marks.
- The exclamation marks produce a very sharp tone which might frighten Grandma. More reassuring language is needed in places.
- The student needs to begin the letter with 'Dear Grandma'.

Makes reader think how nice this would be.

Makes reader feel lonely and afraid.

Makes reader imagine the fire engine, and so the fire.

> Dear Grandma,
> I have been thinking about the fact that you are not as safe and cosy in your home as you might be. I am concerned about the dark and lonely nights. I worry about fire whenever I hear a fire engine's sirens. Please listen to the suggestions I have to make.

Grade C

Good Points

- Emotive language and precise details make the reader picture things happening and feel afraid.
- The student uses a caring tone, which is suitable for the audience (Grandma).
- The writing includes persuasion from the start.

67

Examples and anecdotes

- Develop the points you are making by **giving examples**.

- **Include an anecdote**. Anecdotes are like very short stories which prove your point. Writing about what has actually happened can be very convincing.

The Grade C student is now writing about Grandma's security measures:

An example develops the main point made in the first sentence.

> You need to have more security around you to be safe. For example, when we moved into our new house, Dad fitted new door locks and a chain and we felt better immediately. At the moment you aren't protected against thieves, so anyone could break in. Last year when my friend's parents woke up to find a burglar in their bedroom, it terrified them. I wouldn't want you to go through that.

Anecdote gives a 'real' example of something that has happened.

Good Points

- The general statement ('You need to have more security') is followed by precise detail (the example).
- The anecdote develops and illustrates the point being made.

Rhetoric

- **Rhetoric** is 'language used for effect'. Using rhetoric when writing to persuade will gain you extra marks.

- Some good **rhetorical techniques** are:
  - **imagery** (similes and metaphors): to paint a picture in the reader's mind, e.g.

  you are as valuable to us as the crown jewels

  - **exaggeration**: overstating a view to impress the audience, e.g.

  every day you are in danger …

  - **contrast**: putting two opposites together to create an effect, e.g.

  we want you to be safe, but we fear constant danger

  - **using 'I', 'we', 'you'**, etc: to make the writing more personal, and address the reader, e.g.

  You have to be safe, so that we can be happy.

  - **repetition**: repeating the same word or phrase, e.g.

  we want you safe from burglars, and we want you safe from all other dangers

  - **rhetorical questions**: to challenge the reader, e.g.

  Is there any reason why you shouldn't make these improvements straight away?

  - **humour**: to win the reader over to your view, e.g.

  Don't forget, you have to be perfectly safe so you can cook me my tea whenever I'm passing!

Using a range of techniques

This student has tried to use all the techniques covered in this section.

> Write an article for a national newspaper persuading more people to vote.

Rhetorical question creates a powerful opening and demands the reader's attention.

An example is given.

Examples (TV and darts) are given to illustrate the point.

emotive language

emotive language

Grade C

Clear point of view is hammered home by short sentence at end of paragraph.

Emotive language makes you feel for the victims and the simile adds a powerful detail.

Anecdote highlights main point of article.

direct address ('you')

Why everyone should vote

How many times have you heard someone at the bus stop complaining about taxes or transport? These people usually say they don't vote anyway, because it does no good. But if they don't vote, they have no right to complain. It is as simple as that.

Think about people around the world, they would give almost anything to be allowed to vote for what they believe in. They are tortured when they speak out and often die like animals because they can't vote.

In contrast, so many people nowadays choose to ignore the ballot box, saying that it is pointless. They say their vote is meaningless and a waste of time. As if watching television or playing darts in the pub isn't a waste of time. People have given their lives so that we might have the vote, but that means nothing to many people.

A programme on TV looked at government in Africa. There was a man who queued for ten hours to vote and it was the first time he had been able to. It makes you think how different it is in our society.

So when the next election comes around, you should find the time to vote because it represents your right to choose. You should vote if you care about our country.

Good Points
- The text is persuasive throughout.
- A range of techniques is used effectively.
- There is a powerful opening and conclusion.
- Sentences and vocabulary are varied.

Task

Write the script of a talk to be given on radio. Its aim is to persuade the listeners to become more involved in helping charities.

Structure your talk effectively, and include:
- emotive language
- at least one example or anecdote
- rhetoric.

Writing to advise

Key points

- One of the questions in Section B of Paper 1 lets you **write to advise**.

- When you write to advise, you are helping someone **to do something** or **to behave in a particular way**.

- You should **organise**, **plan** and **present your ideas**.

- You should use the **right tone**, offer **solutions** to the problems and use **examples**.

Organising your ideas

- There are **two methods** you can use when organising your ideas. You could:

  1 First set out a problem in a lot of detail, e.g. how problems with parents can become very serious, **then** offer advice , e.g. how to avoid these problems.

  OR

  2 Set out the advice **as you go**. For each problem, offer some advice, e.g.

  The first thing you mention in your letter is …   *I think that you need to tackle this in three different ways …*

  You then go on to explain that …   *In this particular case, you might consider …*

  Then, there is your concern about …   *If I were you, I would …*

- Make sure you choose **one** of these methods and stick to it. Don't mix the two together.

Planning

- If your advice is logical, it will be convincing. To make your advice logical you need to:

  1 show **what the problem involves**

  2 explain **what can be done about it**.

- Make sure that you cover both these things in your **planning**. A good plan will include ideas of **problems**, and ideas of possible **solutions**.

- This Grade C student was asked to write a section of the school brochure, offering advice to new students about settling in at school. This was her plan. Note the problems, followed by the ideas about solutions.

PLAN

Intro: outline of all the problems
    complicated timetable, big school, confusing layout, moving
    each lesson, masses of students and teachers
Para 2: how to understand the timetable
    why it's necessary, use student planner
Para 3: how to find your way around
    map in planner and on corridors, asking for help
Para 4: how to cope with students
    avoid bullies, get help from form tutor
Para 5: how to cope with teachers
    obey the rules, show respect
Conclusion:

Good Points

- The plan is logical. Problems are briefly outlined in the introduction, then each one is given its own paragraph.
- Advice is offered at each stage ('how to …').

Presenting your ideas

- You may be asked to present your advice in a **particular form**, e.g. a letter, leaflet, advice sheet, speech, magazine article.

- Think about how your **presentation suits the form**. For example, an advice sheet will include **subheadings** to break up the text.

- You could also include **numbers**, **flowcharts** or **bullet points**.

Top Tip!

Don't waste time adding graphics, logos or other illustrations to your answer. You will only earn marks for the *words* you use, and the way you structure your response.

For example:

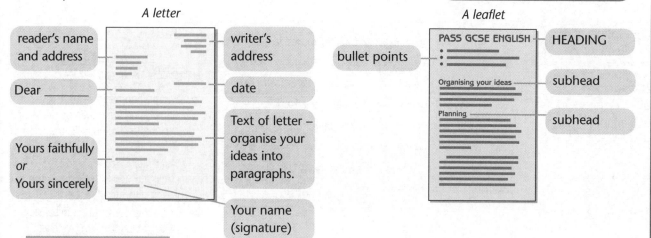

A letter

reader's name and address

Dear _____

Yours faithfully or Yours sincerely

writer's address

date

Text of letter – organise your ideas into paragraphs.

Your name (signature)

A leaflet

PASS GCSE ENGLISH — HEADING

bullet points

Organising your ideas — subhead

Planning — subhead

The right tone

- As with all your writing, make sure the tone suits the **purpose** and **audience**. You need to **address the reader** from the outset, and keep the reader in mind the whole time.

- Use different words and phrases to **vary your tone**:

  – **Commands** tell the reader directly what to do. (Be careful not to use too many though, or you might sound a bit harsh.)

  Take the first chance you get …

  Ask the teacher …

  Don't forget your planner …

  – **'Must'** and **'should'** also make it sound really important that the reader does what you are saying:

  You must learn from others …

  You should not be late …

  – **Softer words** to use are 'can', 'may', 'might' or 'could':

  You could ask a teacher …

  You might like to put your planner …

  – **'If … (then) …'** sets out the result of taking advice (you don't have to include the word 'then'):

  If you adopt a positive attitude, (then) …

- This extract from a Grade C response includes some of these different ways of giving advice.

Don't worry when you come to our school. You need to get to grips with a whole new situation, including the crowds, the size of the school and all the new people. Take a deep breath but try not to panic. If you keep your cool, you will soon get used to it all.

Good Points

- The commands offer clear advice.
- The other approaches have a softer tone. They will make the newcomer more confident.
- The mix of the two approaches makes the writing varied.

TYPES OF WRITING

Offering solutions

- As part of your advice, you need to **offer solutions** to the problems.

The plan on pages 70–71 is for an answer that sets out the advice as it goes along.
Each section, therefore, needs:
- a **description** of the problem
- suggested **solutions**, explaining why they will be effective.

This extract deals with the problem of understanding the school timetable:

description of the problem

first solution offered, plus explanation (because ...)

second solution offered, plus explanation (so ...)

> You will have to cope with strange lesson times, which vary each day. I suggest you always wear a watch, because that will help you to avoid becoming totally confused. You could also look at the timetable in your planner, which gives you the times of each lesson, so you will know exactly where you ought to be and when.

Grade C

Good Points

- The paragraph is set out very clearly: problem, solution 1 + explanation, solution 2 + explanation.
- What needs to be done is straightforward and logical: use a watch and the planner.
- The advice is given in a soft tone ('I suggest you ...', 'you could also ...'), to give the reader confidence.

Using examples

- You can make your advice more convincing by **using examples**:

  Think about what happened when ...

  It is worth remembering ...

Examples link your advice to what has happened in the past. This reassures the reader.
The advice seems easier to trust.

This is how you could **conclude**:

example which looks back to previous successes

makes advice sound easy to follow

> If you accept the advice offered in this booklet you should be fine. Other students who have followed this advice have settled down within a week or so. One said last year: 'I've only been here two weeks, and it feels like home already.' All you need to do is what others have done before you.
>
> So make every effort to blend in, work hard and your future should be rosy.

Grade C

quotation to support the point being made

Top Tip!

Think about adding some quotations from other people to back up the points you are making. They make your answer more varied, too.

enthusiastic final sentence

Using a range of techniques

Try to use all the techniques dealt with in this section, as in the answer below.

> Write an article for a travel magazine, to advise travellers on how to cope with foreign languages.

Grade C

Appropriate tone for this sort of magazine article: it interests and entertains.

The British speak English and expect the rest of the world to do the same. If some foreigner does not speak English, then we shout at him, and he will get the idea!

Ideas organised logically. The old situation is described in paragraph 1, the new approach in paragraph 2.

Why you will benefit.

But most of the British who go abroad now realise that they have to speak a bit of the 'lingo' to get the most out of their time. They can then get on better with the locals and feel as if they have really been somewhere foreign. They can feel less like people on holiday and more like people travelling.

First definite advice: 'if you're sensible' softens the tone.

It is hard to do this straight off, so if you're sensible you need to do some work at home. Language guides are a great start. It is amazing how good you feel if you can ask for bread or order a drink in another language. My brother, who is only seven, loved going to the bakery when we were in France and ordering bread for breakfast. He always came back smiling.

Positive comment: benefits are pointed out.

Example proves the point.

sound piece of advice

You could learn from the signs around you, from menus and just from what you hear in the street. You could ask people what they call knives and forks etc. They will even teach you whole sentences once you show an interest – and you can pick it up really quickly.

Appropriate examples given.

Persuasive conclusion: clever use of language makes the advice more acceptable.

It is simply a matter of making the effort and then enjoying the results. Travel broadens the mind, they say – it can also broaden your language skills!

Can you understand English??!!!

Good Points ✓

- The response presents situations, offers solutions and suggests likely outcomes.
- The tone is light but presents some serious points.
- The examples give the advice more credibility.
- The introduction and conclusion are memorable.
- The answer develops logically.
- Language is used effectively.

Task

Your school has been given a grant of £100,000 from the government. On behalf of your year group, write a letter to your headteacher to offer advice on how the school should spend it.

Writing to inform

Key points

- One of the questions in Section B of Paper 2 lets you **write to inform**.
- The information should be **clear**, **detailed** and **relevant**.
- **Organise your ideas** well.
- Include **facts** and **opinions**.
- Add **personal feelings and experiences** to gain extra marks.

Top Tip!

It is much better to write in depth about a few points than to try to cover everything in a very general way. Try to focus on the most important points and include as much detail as possible.

Choosing the information

- Information texts aim to tell someone about something.
- Begin by **planning**. Jot down your ideas in brief, as in this **spider diagram**.

> Write a letter to a pen friend who is about to visit from abroad, to tell them about the area in which you live.

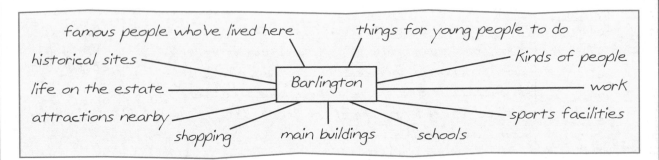

famous people who've lived here   things for young people to do

historical sites —

life on the estate —

attractions nearby —

shopping   main buildings   schools

Barlington

Kinds of people

work

sports facilities

- Now decide which are the **most important** points, and focus on those.

Organising your ideas

- Organise your points so that similar ideas are covered at the same time.
- Look at the detailed plan below. Each main topic is given a new paragraph. A few significant points of information are covered in each topic.

Introduction gives summary.	**PLAN** Intro: general details looking forward to the visit, much to find out about, many things to see
Begins close to home.	Para 2: what is nearby neighbours, the estate – shops and houses
Moves out to wider town.	Para 3: the town employment, schools, facilities

Then mentions other interesting features.	Para 4: what's worth seeing
	   historical sites, buildings, attractions
	Para 5: other points of interest
	   youth culture, recent improvements

Ends with summary.	Conclusion: summary of Barlington some fun, some interest

Good Points

- Most of the ideas in the spider diagram are included in this detailed plan.
- They are organised into particular topics, one per paragraph.
- There is a logical development: introduction – nearby – town itself – famous features – other points of interest – summary.

Facts and opinions

- Make sure you include a mixture of facts and opinions.
  - The **facts** provide the basic detail.
  - The **opinions** tell the reader what you think about the information. Opinions give it a more personal focus.

This student has provided a mixture of facts and opinions in her **introduction**.

> Dear Gabbi,
>
> We are really looking forward to your visit. I thought I would tell you all about where we live, so there will be no surprises when you arrive. There are many good things here. We are surrounded by history, which can be quite fascinating. Also, there are some unusual things. Some of the families around us seem a bit odd, but they aren't dangerous!

Top Tip!

Remember:
Facts are things that we know are true, e.g. information about when a building was built.
Opinions are what the writer believes or feels about the facts, e.g. whether s/he likes the building.

Pages 8–9

Good Points ✔

- Student includes some **facts** – what she is going to do; the place is full of history.
- The **opinions** make it more personal – 'good things', 'fascinating', 'unusual', 'odd'.

Making the information clear

- When you write to inform, you must make the **information clear**. Assume that the reader knows nothing about what you are describing.
- The **more detail** you can give, the clearer your information will be.
- **Link the paragraphs** to show how all the information connects together.

The letter to Gabbi needs to be absolutely clear, because she probably has no knowledge of the local area.

Links with previous paragraph.

Details make information clear and interesting.

Further detail given.

> We do, though, have some attractions which you will find interesting. My parents plan to take us to the castle, which is in all the history books. It was the site of a famous battle during the Wars of the Roses and I think in the Civil War too. From the top, you get great views of the countryside around. You can almost imagine the soldiers fighting and dying as you watch from the walls. The museum there shows many of the weapons and tells you more about how the battles were organised ...

Grade C

personal opinion

Personal response – she paints a picture of her watching from the castle.

Good Points ✔

- The detail and personal response bring the facts about the castle to life.
- The paragraph has been linked to the one before.

TYPES OF WRITING

Personal response

- Try to provide a **personal response**. That means including your **feelings** about things. Referring to your own experience is much more powerful than just providing a list of details.

- It is especially important to give your personal response in your **conclusion**. When you sum up for the reader you should give your own view about the information.

This is how one student ended the letter to her friend:

> You will be able to experience the things I have told you about, and give us your opinions on them. Personally, I am certain you will enjoy the sports facilities best – but we will see whether I am right.
> Best wishes ...

Grade D

This makes a more effective ending:

Grade C

Shows that you are summing up.

Note variety of sentence types, and use of adjectives to add colour and detail.

> You should now have a good picture of what it is like here and we hope you will have a wonderful time while you are with us. You will be given a really warm welcome. I can promise you many things to do: guided tours of our historical buildings, fun afternoons at the sports centre, and great evenings with my crazy friends.
>
> To complete your 'English' holiday you will be treated to a huge helping of fish and chips at the local chippy, which will give you something to remember when you get home!

Final example of what the area has to offer, and personal opinion on the effect it will have.

Good Points ✓

- The response gives a personal view but is still informative.
- The writer's opinion suggests it will all be enjoyable.
- The sentences and the use of language are varied.
- The letter comes to an effective ending, by imagining the last day and the guest returning home.

Top Tip!

Remember to make your information writing lively and interesting:
- Use different lengths and types of sentence.

Pages 54–55

- Use colourful or powerful words instead of plain, general words.

Pages 56–57

Using a range of techniques

Try to use all the techniques dealt with in this section, as in the answer below.

Write an article for a national newspaper, to inform the readers about the problems faced by modern teenagers.

1st paragraph links with title and briefly covers all the topics. Shows good planning.

2nd paragraph covers topic of being treated like children. Detailed examples are given of life at home.

3rd paragraph covers topic of life outside the home. This is made clear in the link 'outside the home'.

4th paragraph covers topic of school. Note link words 'at school' and varied sentence structure.

5th paragraph sums up problems and gives contrast with older people.

Grade C

It has never been easy to be a teenager, and it is very difficult today. The world expects us to be grown up but we aren't treated like adults. We live in a dangerous society, for example where drugs are readily available. At school we have exam after exam and we have to cope with growing up as well, so it's hardly any wonder that we struggle at times.

One of the biggest problems is that adults want us to be mature but they still treat us like children. We help around the house, but we're told to come back by a certain time at night. We are expected to get a part-time job to earn money, but we don't have a say about where we go for the family holiday.

Outside the home, there are dangers everywhere. Older people had alcohol and cigarettes, that's true, but it was easy by comparison. We go to a club, then are faced with drug dealers and pressure from friends and our own need to fit in with the crowd. Then there are all the designer clothes that tempt us too. Being a teenager has never been harder.

At school we have so many exams, it is difficult to keep track: SATs, GCSEs, coursework, mocks .... We get homework every night. The teachers work us harder and harder because they have to improve results or their own careers will suffer.

And teenagers are suffering from hormones, relationship problems, and changes in their bodies. I suppose our parents and grandparents suffered the same, but they didn't have all the other modern pressures we have. They are lucky they were born at another time.

Good Points

- The writer presents detailed information in an organised way.
- The facts are supported and illustrated by opinions.
- The language and style suit the purpose and audience of the task.

Task

Write informatively about a pastime you enjoy.

Note: In a task of this kind, you should assume your audience is the examiner.

Writing to explain

Key points

- One of the questions in Section B of Paper 2 lets you **write to explain**.

- Explaining is **different from just giving information**.

- Writing to explain requires:

  – good **structure** and **planning**

  – content which sets out **how or why** something occurs, rather than just what happens

  – clear but interesting **language**.

Top Tip!

Many students lose marks because they don't *explain* the subject they are writing about. Examiners will be looking for explanation. Don't just write information.

Structure and planning

- Explaining something means helping someone understand. Your structure has to be clear. This means paying special attention to your planning.

Think about this title:

> Most people have memories of a particular holiday or trip.
> Choose one that you have experienced, and explain why it was so memorable.

Top Tip!

This question does *not* ask you to:
- write about trips in general
- describe what happened on one special trip
- write a lot of information about the place you visited.

It *does* ask you to:
- decide what made one trip special and say why
- select memorable features of the trip and explain why they are memorable.

Your plan might look like this:

PLAN

Intro: where we went, why memorable
         Turkey, highs and lows
Para 2: first part fun
         beaches, food, friends: show why
Para 3: dad's nightmare
         drunken evening, people complaining,
         explain what happened
Para 4: mum bitten by cat
         rabies fears, hospital, how it went from
         bad to worse
Para 5: leaving
         people friendly: explain it still didn't
         take away the horror
Conclusion: never going back!
         problems bigger than pleasures

Top Tip!

Choose only a few points to write about. It is better to explain a few points in detail, rather than trying to include too much material.

Good Points

- The plan is organised clearly. The introduction shows two sides to the holiday. More detail is given in the following paragraphs.
- There is a focus on explanation throughout: 'why', 'explain', and 'how' are all important words in this plan.

OR:

You could plan by linking some text bubbles like this. (The main point is inside the bubble. The lines branching off each bubble give examples or go into more detail. They develop the main point.)

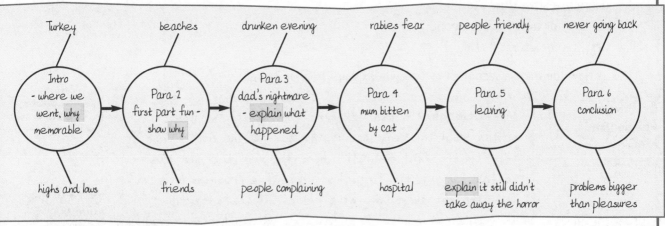

Turkey

beaches

drunken evening

rabies fear

people friendly

never going back

Intro
- where we went, why memorable

Para 2
first part fun - show why

Para 3
dad's nightmare - explain what happened

Para 4
mum bitten by cat

Para 5
leaving

Para 6
conclusion

highs and lows

friends

people complaining

hospital

explain it still didn't take away the horror

problems bigger than pleasures

Introduction

- It is a good idea to **explain from the beginning** of your answer. This shows the examiner that you are not just writing information or description. It will also help to keep you focused on the task.

Look at how these students approach the task differently:

About six years ago, I went on holiday with my family to Turkey. We wanted to go to Turkey for years, and finally we were there. We stayed in a place called Datca, it was on the coast and very hot. And there were not many British people there. We had some good times and some bad times and I am going to tell you about the bad times.

Grade D

How To Improve

- There is a clear first sentence, setting the scene, but the student does not explain why it was a memorable holiday.
- It is treated more like an information text ('I am going to tell you').

About six years ago, I went on holiday with my family to Turkey. We stayed in a place called Datca, and there were not many British people there. I am sure we could have had a good time and then it would have been 'just another holiday'. However, there were also some seriously bad moments which made the holiday especially memorable.

Grade C

Good Points

- It gives clear background information.
- Then it implies it was special – not 'just another holiday'.
- It refers to the key word in the question – 'memorable'.
- Begins to explain and focuses on the title.

Top Tip!

Even if you are asked to write about your own experiences, you don't have to tell a true story. You can either make it up altogether, or base the story on something that happened. Whichever you do, you need to make it believable.

TYPES OF WRITING

'How' and 'why'

- When you write to explain, you are **giving reasons**, saying **why** or **how** something happens (or happened).

- A good way of doing this is to:
  - describe a **situation**
  - say **why** or **how** it came about
  - describe the **effect** it had.

Look at how the middle section of this answer explains how and why:

Describes the situation and explains how it came about.

> My mother had a real problem. One night, she was bitten by a cat. She had to go to see the doctor and then to the local hospital, where she was told she had to have an injection into her stomach every two days. They thought she might have rabies. This was terrible, and made our holiday a nightmare. My mother was really frightened, and cried quite often. The injections really hurt her, and it is not something we will ever forget.

Grade C

Explains the effect on the family.

Links to the question, explaining why it has made such an impression.

Using the right language

- The explanation must be **clear**, so that the reader understands it perfectly.

- Some **phrases** are useful to make your explanations clear:

1 Phrases to explain **the reasons and causes of something**:

Because   So   Therefore

As a result of this

This meant that

This is because

The reason for this

As a consequence

2 Phrases to show when something is **uncertain**:

It could be

It may be that

It might be that

Perhaps

Top Tip!

- In your conclusion, try to sum up the key points of the explanation. In this case, it would be what made the trip memorable.
- It is also your chance to refer back to the question. This shows you have been focusing on the question throughout, which always impresses the examiner.

Some of these phrases have been used in this conclusion:

'might be' suggests a possible explanation.

> It might be that what happened to my mother has had a real effect on what I think about Turkey. It is a beautiful country, and has friendly people, but my mother had a terrible time, my father was really cut up, and the rest of us just felt helpless. This meant that things we wanted to enjoy, like the beach, were forgotten, and instead we remember the hospital visits. Also, things we laughed about at the time, such as my dad's experience when he got drunk, we couldn't laugh about afterwards. My mother was in pain, so we remember that and nothing else, really.

Grade C

Explains again why the trip was so memorable.

Phrase introduces an explanation.

Still explaining how they were affected.

Good Points

- The holiday is summarised in the conclusion.
- The effects of the bad time are explained: we know why it was so memorable and how they reacted.

Using all the techniques

Try to use all the techniques dealt with in this section, as in the answer below.

Explain what you most dislike about television.

Grade C

Begins with a positive, but then goes on to show the other side.

> I am sure that television is not all bad. However, what is on TV in my house is awful. In fact it kills off brain cells. I am sick of soaps and reality television above all.
>
> Daytime television isn't even worth talking about, it is beneath contempt, but even in the evening the programmes are just boring. The soaps drip on and on, as interesting as watching golf. Everyone in the programme spends every night in the pub having disasters; and we sit on our settees eating our tea and lapping up the rubbish, because there seems to be no alternative.
>
> Unfortunately, reality shows make everything worse. Because they haven't got anything better to do, people sit and watch non-celebrities swearing at each other in the jungle and gossiping about who might fancy who. On the next night, they watch youngsters who are locked in a house together, hoping they might decide to have sex or at least a row.
>
> At times, it's so bad it makes you think that it must have been better to live in a time when families gathered round a piano singing hymns at night. At least life was real then, not like the so-called reality TV shows.
>
> The worst thing about these types of programmes is they stop us thinking. I see it all the time in my family: my brother watches TV all the time and is becoming a vegetable. My sister is so addicted to 'Friends' that life for her stops between 8pm and 9pm. I'm glad I can escape to my room and read a book!

Contrast: explains what he dislikes most; note the exaggeration for effect.

powerful image

Explains problems with evening TV.

Second problem explained.

Why he does not like the programmes – words like 'gossiping' show he is critical.

Explains why we act as we do.

'because' introduces the reason.

sarcasm

Explains it is the unreality of reality TV shows that he dislikes.

'the worst thing ... is ...' shows he is about to give a reason.

Shows how this affects his family, and why it upsets him.

Conclusion: sums up criticism.

Good Points

- The introduction introduces two features of TV which he dislikes.
- The two main dislikes are then explained in detail in separate paragraphs.
- The answer concentrates on 'why' and 'how' rather than just 'what'.
- The language is entertaining in places (e.g. 'the soaps drip on and on'), and includes sarcasm.
- There is a good attempt to vary sentence structure.

Task

Explain how you have dealt with difficult situations that have arisen in your life.
You might wish to write about:

- relationships with parents
- friends and their expectations
- problems at school
- any other difficult situations you have met.

Writing to describe

Key points

- One of the questions in Section B of Paper 2 lets you **write to describe**.

- You will probably have to describe a **person or place**.

- When writing to describe, you should:
  - describe what you know
  - plan and structure the description
  - write an effective introduction and conclusion
  - use your five senses, as appropriate
  - go into detail.

> **Top Tip!**
>
> The aim of descriptive writing is to give the reader a clear picture of the person or place you are describing. It is very unlikely that you will be asked to write a story.

Describe what you know

- Describe something or someone **you really know about**. You may think it is more interesting to describe someone from Siberia, but your lack of knowledge will show in the writing.

- If you invent a **person**, base them on someone (or some people) you know well. He or she will then come across as a real person.

- If you are describing a **place**, choose one where you have lived, or one you have visited.

Structure

- **Group your ideas** together in a plan. Unless you plan carefully, your description will ramble and have no structure.

This is a **plan** for a response to the question: 'Describe a beach in August.'. The main ideas have each been given a separate paragraph. The further details show how the ideas can be developed.

> PLAN
>
> Intro:
>   the overall atmosphere on beach
> Para 2: families
>   dads red, mothers looking after babies and youngsters
> Para 3: children
>   on sands, in sea, ice cream, sunburn
> Para 4: sea
>   sandy grey waves, seaweed, lilos
> Conclusion:
>   view from the pier, people drifting to steps and home

>  **Good Points**
>
> - The plan is clearly divided into sections.
> - Some ideas for developing the main points are given in each section.

Introduction

- A **lively opening** will immediately attract the examiner's attention.

> When I arrived at the beach, it was busy and exciting. Families in bright T-shirts were packed together, music blared and children were screaming. The sun beat down and the waves lapped against the shore.

Grade C

Good Points

- It is clear from the start what the student is writing about.
- Sounds, as well as sights, are described.
- The beach and the people are both described.
- Interesting words are used ('packed', 'blared', 'lapped').

Top Tip!

For a really striking opening, think about a different approach, e.g.
- Focus on one family in detail.
- Focus on one particular area, then broaden out.
- Begin with someone speaking.

Include all five senses and detail

- Good descriptive writing usually appeals to **all five senses**. Write about what you (or other people) are seeing, hearing, touching/feeling, smelling and tasting.

- The more **detail** you include, the better the description. Describe a particular beach towel, for example, not just beach towels in general.

Note how this extract uses the techniques above.

Top Tip!

If you are writing a description of a person, don't include all the senses. Instead, try to include some description of background, such as the things they like to do.

sight

taste

feeling

> The coloured windbreaks and T-shirts were bright. You could smell sun-tan cream and fried onions from hot-dog stalls, and your lips tasted of salt and sand. All along the beach, the fathers sat in deck chairs, reading their newspapers with sweat running down their necks or lay on towels. The mothers tried to make the children behave properly, shouting at boys and girls, who were shouting back. One woman in a Liverpudlian accent was screaming, and looked set to explode.

Grade C

smell

sound

Top Tip!

Good descriptive writing often includes features that are found in poetry. For example, you could include a simile such as 'fathers sat in deck chairs, going red like apples in the sun'.

Good Points

- All the senses are used to help the reader experience the seaside.
- There is some good detail, such as 'fried onions from hot-dog stalls'.

TYPES OF WRITING

Conclusions

- Your conclusion should **round off the writing**. Don't let it just tail off.

- Try to **link** your final paragraph in some way with the introduction. Go back and read the introduction before you write your conclusion.

Look at how this student ends her response:

'Now' shows that we have moved on to a different time.

Shows how the people are moving away.

> Now, it is cooler in the evening sun. The sand is mixed with litter and the sandcastles are broken down. Families are heading home. They queue at the steps to leave the beach. The children are tired and quiet, and parents carry bags and towels. The tide is coming in again, and soon it will be cleaning all the mess away.

Grade C

Shows how the beach has changed.

Hints at what will happen soon.

Good Points ✔

- A good description, which describes the weather, the beach and the people.
- This final paragraph links effectively with the introduction: time has moved on.
- Details show how things have changed, e.g. the children are quiet now.

Using a range of techniques

Try to use all the techniques dealt with in this section, as in the answer below.

> Describe a person who inspires you.

Contrast makes an effective introduction.

Detail – name of hospital makes it real.

> Some people choose sportsmen or soldiers as their heroes. However, the person who inspires me is not famous, he goes to the same school. His name is Jonathon and he is paralysed from the waist down.
>
> Before he was injured he was very well built – and according to most girls, he was the Brad Pitt of Year 11. He was captain of the football team and Head Boy of the school. Then, just before his mock A levels, he went downhill on a sledge in the snow and hit a tree. When he woke up, he was in the serious injuries unit in Stoke Mandeville Hospital, and was told he might never feel any movement below his neck again.
>
> He did, though. He wanted so badly to get better and be mobile. He did not want to be looked after for the rest of his life. He had too much living still to do.

Grade C

Description of his looks and abilities.

Description of his attitude – note short sentence for surprise effect at start of paragraph.

Describes his intelligence.

Now, he goes round in his wheelchair like a racing driver and does wheelies all the time at parties. Although he's missed so many months, he's going to pass all his exams with A grades, and should get a good university place. He might not ever be able to play rugby but he will make an excellent doctor, which is what he wants to do.

humorous simile

He must lie awake at night and be very upset. Still, his arms are becoming stronger, he wants to complete a wheelchair marathon and convinces you that he will do it. He will not accept his life has been ended by being in a wheelchair.

Conclusion returns to the idea of being an 'everyday' hero.

Because of all this, Jonathon is greater than Wayne Rooney or Neil Armstrong or anyone else I have ever heard of. He is so normal, but also so different. He convinces you that he can do anything he sets his mind on and he's a great inspiration to us all.

Top Tip!

When describing someone, you usually give your own views. You could add variety and interest by including:
- a conversation with them – to highlight how they talk or think
- someone else's view of them.

Good Points ✓

- The response is well structured. Each paragraph describes a different aspect of Jonathon.
- Some detail and interesting words are used.
- Clear sentence structure with some powerful short sentences for effect.
- There is an effective introduction, which is referred to in the conclusion.
- The writing shows the student's feelings about Jonathon.

Combining types of writing

- An option in Section B for both Papers is to write a response which involves more than one kind of writing. For example:
  - A question on Paper 1 might ask you to argue, persuade and advise.
  - A question on Paper 2 might require an answer that describes and explains.

- Any combination of writing skills is possible. You can use the skills you have learnt for each type of writing to cover all the types of writing that the question is asking for. For lots of practice questions, you can use *Easy Learning GCSE English Foundation & Higher Exam Practice Workbook for AQA A*.

Task

Describe a place where you spend much of your time, for example:
- a park
- a swimming pool
- a club
- your bedroom.

Raising your grade

Key points

If you want to raise your grade to C or above, you need to show these skills. All extracts are from a response to the question on the right:

> Write an article for a national newspaper in which you argue that parents should or should not be held responsible for the actions of their children.

Purpose and audience

- Think hard about the **purpose** and **audience** of the task before and during writing.
- For example, if the **purpose** of the task is to argue or explain, don't inform or describe.
- Make sure the **form** of the writing suits the purpose, e.g. a letter, speech, advice leaflet.
- Think about the **audience** – what kind of language and style would suit them?

> It is crazy that parents should be punished if their sons or daughters truant from school. After all, when someone becomes a teenager, they know what they want to do – and they do it, whatever their parents say.

Clear argument shows a strong sense of purpose. The formal style suits the audience (newspaper readers).

Structure and planning

- Make sure you do a **plan** before you begin writing.
- Use **paragraphs** to organise your writing: a new paragraph for each new point or idea.
- **Develop the points** in your paragraphs, and use words like 'however' and 'next day' to connect them.

> Mind you, some people say that if children are brought up properly, there won't be a problem and it's down to the parents from the start. But it's not as simple as that ...

New paragraph to present the opposing argument. 'But...' shows how the next idea counters this.

Make your writing more exciting

- Grab the **reader's interest** and keep it, for example by using quotations, anecdotes (stories), examples and humour.
- Use **interesting vocabulary** wherever you can. Go back and change words when you are checking your work.
- **Vary** the length and structure of your **sentences**. Use different kinds of sentence (e.g. questions, exclamations).

> Imagine, for example, how a parent might have to struggle if a 16-year-old refuses to go to school. What is the mother supposed to do? Does she stop his sweety money? Of course she can't.

Variety of types of sentence, and lengths of sentence. The questions get the reader's attention. 'how a parent struggles' is more interesting vocabulary than 'what a parent does'.

Punctuation, grammar and spelling

- Use **punctuation** to control your sentences.
- Make your **grammar** as accurate as you can.
- Try to spell accurately.

> You can bring your kids up really well, but if they make some bad friends they are led astray easily, like when they are out on the streets.

Note the commas used to separate the parts of the sentence.

Read the question and an extract from a student's answer below.
The notes show why the examiner awarded it a C grade.

We usually know most about those closest to us. Write a **description** of a member of your family.

Links to what has gone before.

Grade C

> However, when he was younger, he was very different. You can see it in old photographs and my father has told me a lot about him. He was wild and used to go round with gangs of 'rockers', as they were called. Sometimes he would get into fights. Once he even ended up in hospital.
>
> He used to ride an old motorbike that was always breaking down and he would get home late and covered in oil. He never seemed to mind though, and perhaps that is why he eventually ended up opening the garage and working there all hours of the day and night.
>
> He is happy there. As he once said to me; 'Where else can you mess around with engines and get covered in mess and get paid for it? It's brilliant.' That is how he sees the job and because he enjoys it so much, lots of people take their cars to him to be fixed. He is a very popular mechanic.
>
> At home, he spends a lot of time in the garden. That's not because he likes gardening, it's because my Auntie Sylvia makes him go out there, to get him out from under her feet. He spends a lot of time in his shed and we aren't sure what he does there really . . .

Punctuation used accurately: here, inverted commas.

Keeps up the interest by adding detail.

Quotation brings character to life.

different types of sentences

humour

Purpose is clear throughout: tight focus on uncle.

- The response gives a clear picture of the man. It is in an appropriate style for the audience – in this case, the examiner. There are attempts to engage the reader's interest, for example the quotation and the touch of humour in the final paragraph. The paragraphs are well linked and the writing is mostly accurate.

Answers

Reading media and non-fiction

Remember that there are no 'right or wrong' answers in English, as there are in Maths or Science. The answers below are only examples of Grade C responses. Compare them with your own answers: if yours contain similar features, then you are working at Grade C level. If your answers don't seem as good, then ask yourself how you can improve them.

page 9
Grade C

The first text relies heavily on opinions, for example 'Sharon's going to cause a lot of trouble' and she is called 'mouthy'. These opinions make us think badly about Sharon even before we have seen her: they turn us against her but also make us interested in watching. And this is why the opinions are given, because the purpose of the text is to make us watch the programme.

The second text, by contrast, begins with facts. Because it is a newspaper report, it sets out exactly what is happening: who is collecting money and why. The report ends by printing the facts about the problems of Africa: over 2 million killed because of AIDS, and so on. This is probably to get people to donate money. The opinions in the article come from Graham. He talks about the 'unfair world' and 'injustice'. He says, 'the problems … are hard for us even to imagine,' which is of course his opinion.

In conclusion, the texts are very different, but each suits its purpose. The *Inside Soap* article is mainly aimed at advertising a TV programme so it talks it up. The newspaper article is mainly aimed at reporting factually what Graham and Chris Lingard are doing, and his opinions are part of the story.

page 13
Grade C

The writer fears he is becoming old. He used to like *Top of the Pops* and Tony Blackburn, and now pop music on TV is full of 'semi-naked girls'. So the way things have moved on is really what he is writing about.

He begins by telling you something about himself, so that you know how old he is and how he is a bit worried about this. He is looking forward to watching pop music with his children, but 'shock and dismay' it is totally different now. The son is cool about this but he is horrified, he realises he is heading towards the last stage in his life and even thinks about bingo and stair lifts. At the end he pulls himself together and realises that he must appreciate what he's got now 'while I still can'.

The writer uses lots of techniques to get you on his side. Humour is one, for example 'No drier in the toilets?' And it is funny how he gets so stressed out by the Kiss channel but his son is cool about it. This is also an example of contrast, which he uses a lot as well, for example the *Top of the Pops* DJ was 'friendly, reliable, old', as opposed to the 'semi-naked girls faintly disguised as pop artists'. He also exaggerates a lot, like when he says pop stars have rings all over them like chain mail.

page 17

- **exaggeration**: All eyes turn to the sea
- **simile**: like a satellite
- **direct address to reader**: you'll find
- **list**: Sorrento, Positano, Salerno and Amalfi
- **metaphor**: fleeing across
- **simile**: statues sit like sentinels surveying

page 20

Each column begins in the same way, first with a quote, to show the most important thing that the person thinks about the question. For example the cleaner's quote is 'I work hard because I have no choice'. This is a harsh view of life, which contrasts with the two quotes of the other two people interviewed.

page 23
Grade C

The report comes from a popular newspaper and is against the arrival of the ship. The headline says it is 'a toxic rust-bucket', which turns the reader against it immediately. The word 'protest' in the strapline adds some human interest by showing that it is something that people are up in arms about. The language is powerful throughout the article, for example a 'rusting ghost ship' and 'packed with toxic chemicals'. We aren't just given the facts but there is opinion too. And because the final paragraph is a quote from a protester, we are left with that point of view.

The report is very short, with just one sentence in each paragraph, which makes it easy to read. There is far more space given to the photo and the headlines. There are two headlines and the second one is underlined to make it stand out. The picture is huge to show that the ship is a massive problem, and it looks deliberately old and grey and dangerous. People are shown on the shore, though hardly the crowds mentioned in the article.

page 25

Grade C

The first text does have some facts, such as that Crossley had his first teaching post at Loveridge Primary School, but most of it is opinion. It consists of Crossley telling a story about how he got the attention of the class. When someone is telling a story from long ago you cannot tell how truthful it is. And it includes a lot of exaggeration, such as 'nervous wreck' and 'transfixed'.

Text 2 is different because it is full of facts. The first sentence tells us the facts that Frank is 78 and that he lives on the Albany Estate. Later on it gives details of what the gangs have done to him. However, some of the words used make us feel strongly about the situation, such as 'prisoner in his house'. This is the opinion of the writer, who could have said 'Frank hasn't wanted to leave his house'. Also, Frank's own opinion is given at the end.

The two texts have different audiences, which explains why their use of fact and opinion is different. Text 1 is read by teachers who want to hear a lovely story. Text 2 is from a newspaper, so people want the facts above all, but they also want to feel strongly about the story, so there are opinions as well.

Reading poems from different cultures and traditions

page 29

There are no 'correct' answers: any two poems are acceptable, as long as you have a clear idea about how they both focus on the theme in the question. All the poems below come from the first eight poems of the Anthology (Cluster 1), but you can compare poems from either cluster in your exam answer. The following list is just a starting point for your revision.

Suffering

Limbo – slavery
What Were They Like? – contrast between peaceful life and war
Others possible: *Night of the Scorpion, Blessing, Nothing's Changed*

Poverty

Night of the Scorpion – family living conditions
Blessing – lack of water
Others possible: *Nothing's Changed, Two Scavengers in a Truck*

Inequality

Nothing's Changed – contrasts between whites and blacks
Two Scavengers in a Truck – totally different lifestyles
Other possible: *Limbo*

Man and Nature

Vultures – linked through love and evil
What Were They Like? – what the war did to the country
Others possible: *Blessing, Night of the Scorpion, Island Man*

Contrasting cultures

Island Man – differences between past and present
Two Scavengers in a Truck – the rich and poor
Others possible: *Nothing's Changed*, any contrast between the cultures presented in the poems

page 31

Extract from a Grade C response

… The society we see in *Two Scavengers in a Truck* is one that is in parts. On one side there are the scavengers, but they are on a garbage truck and they are separated from the richer people:

> 'looking down into
>
> an elegant open Mercedes'.

The gulf between them and the rich is significant. Both sets of people are at the same stop light but have no real connection – the couple in the elegant car do not even seem to cast a glance at the poorer scavengers.

We see a similar society in South Africa in *Nothing's Changed*. There, the whites have a smart new restaurant: 'new, up-market, haute cuisine', while the poor blacks have to make do with a 'working man's café'.

In this case, we do not see the whites with the advantages, but we learn about the world in which they live, which has:

> 'ice white glass,
> linen falls,
> the single rose'.

This is made to appear very beautiful, and is a contrast to the world of the working blacks:

> 'wipe your fingers on your jeans,
> spit a little on the floor:
> it's in the bone.'

The poet is speaking sarcastically. If people behave badly, it is because of the conditions. Probably the scavengers do not want to look 'grungy' either, but in both cases they have no real choice: this is their life, whilst others have all the advantages …

page 35

Extract from a Grade C response

The poem is set in a hot country, where the people are poor and there is little water. When the pipe bursts and water shoots out, they become excited and rush out to collect it in anything they can. The children play in it, though.

The poet has sympathy with these people. She understands that they are always short of water:
    'There never is enough water.'

She describes the effects, as 'skin cracks like a pod'. She shows how they dream of water: 'Imagine the drip of it'. She describes it in religious language (e.g. 'kindly god', 'blessing'), which shows it is important to them. In fact, the water is seen as 'fortune', 'silver' and 'liquid sun'. It is very valuable.

The message of the poem is that sometimes things can be better. Yes the people fight for the water but that's because of how desperate they are. The children are happy when the water 'sings' over them. Though we finish with an image of their 'small bones' which makes us think they are weak and it won't be long before there is no water again.

Yet this is still much more positive than the message in *Not my Business*, because here the suffering has no break. It reveals endless violence in a society. Dharker sees the problem as one of climate and a lack of water, but Osundare sees the problem in evil people.

page 37

Extract from a Grade C response

The poem is set out in two sections. The first section has a series of questions about the people of Viet Nam. The second section answers them. The questions suggest the Vietnamese are artistic people – or rather were, because it suggests that so many have been killed. For example:
    'Did they use bone and ivory,
    jade and silver, for ornament?'

The answers are unpleasant – for example, 'Sir, their light hearts turned to stone'. Each answer shows how their life and culture were destroyed: 'Sir, laughter is bitter to the burned mouth.'

The poem moves towards the final ending of death – 'It is silent now.' This is because their culture, traditions and happiness have all gone.

So the poem has a strange structure but the reason is to make the reader remember all the good things about life in Viet Nam before the war. Then the answers show how the terrible war has affected the country. The structure is effective, because the questions describe a beautiful world, where the Vietnamese are happy, then the second section shatters this dream. Also, it's like someone asking the reader questions, so it's direct.

page 41

Extract from a Grade C response

Dharker begins with metaphors of hatching ('breaking out' and 'cracking'), which suggests new growth. There is then a list of open things: 'space, light, / empty air'.

The words suggest things going upwards, and the sound effects such as the use of 'c's emphasises the amazing scene. The climax is 'crash through clouds'.

Alvi, though, is describing a life where she is stuck. She contrasts the softness of the Pakistani clothes ('satin-silken') with the more basic British clothes she really desires: 'denim and corduroy'. The presents are more exotic but she explains in a simile she 'could never be as lovely as those clothes'. She feels out of place between two cultures. She wants to rise out of it like a phoenix (a mythical animal that grew out of the ashes) but cannot.

Dharker's poem is positive, with lots of images of moving upwards and getting brighter. Dharker's life is being re-born, but Alvi is not like a phoenix, she is trapped and she does not seem able to rise out of her frustrating life: 'my costume clung to me'.

page 45

Grade C

Both *Half-Caste* and *from Search For My Tongue* are about people who are uncomfortable in the society where they live. John Agard is angry, because he does not feel 'half' of anything, Sujata Bhatt is worried because she thinks she is losing her mother tongue, through speaking English all day.

Agard demands an explanation for the way people speak to him: 'Explain yuself'. Calling him 'half-caste' is insulting. Because he does not want to be seen as 'half-caste', he gives examples of how colours are mixed – painting and music and weather. Since none of these items are thought of as half-caste, why should it happen to him?

Agard is sarcastic:
    'Excuse me
    standing on one leg
    I'm half-caste'.

He is making fun of those who label him, he demands they come back as whole people to see him:
    'wid de whole of yu ear
    and de whole of yu mind'.

They are the ones who are not proper, complete people. Then, he says, they will learn he is a whole person:
    'an I will tell yu
    de other half
    of my story'.

These final lines are in a stanza on their own, to make them stand out and show how angry the poet is. The poem is about his bitterness about the idea of 'halfness'. The poet deliberately doesn't use much punctuation and use of common speech patterns, but we are meant to notice how intelligent he is too, as he talks about art and music, and his use of long words like 'consequently'.

Bhatt's problem is that she is uncomfortable handling two languages, which represent two cultures. Since she speaks in a foreign tongue she thinks her mother tongue could die. She believes it dies and rots, and she spits it out and thinks she is left with only the new language.

Since she uses the metaphor of a flower to talk about her language, it shows she thinks it is delicate and beautiful. Then she reveals that the tongue, like a plant, grows back in the night. It seems to be the better language, because she says 'it ties the other tongue in knots'. She sounds delighted at the end, when the mother tongue 'blossoms'.

Bhatt's feelings, like Agard's, are also shown successfully. Her mother tongue is used in the poem to show the reader what she dreams (in Gujerati). This shows us how difficult it must be to live with a difficult second language. How relieved Bhatt is when her tongue survives is cleverly shown as it grows from a rotten leftover, to a stump, up to a bud, then a flower which blossoms. The poem begins with her unhappiness at having lost her tongue, but ends with her recovering it.

Writing

page 51

1 the text of a speech (form/purpose)
your year group (audience)
inform (purpose)
what the school offers out of lesson time (content)

2 For example:

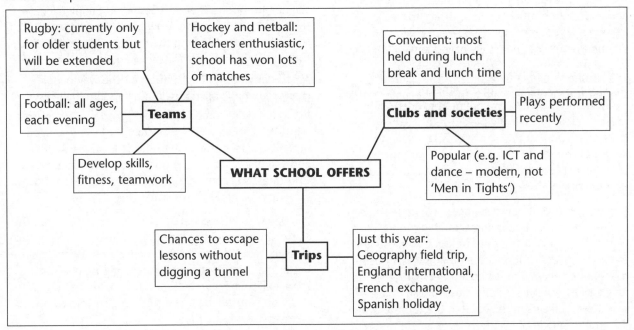

page 55

Castle World is your once-in-a-lifetime chance to go back in time. You can be a knight for a whole day, or you can be a servant in the fabulous great hall. The amazing rides and activities are so stunning that you will want to stay in the Middle Ages instead of going home.

page 57

At home, Uncle Tom seems to spend countless hours locked in his study. This isn't because he enjoys marking mountains of school books ... no, it's to escape from the dreaded Aunt Sylvia. Another escape route is school, 3 miles down the road, where he often works late into the evening.

page 59

1 Jake's guitar teacher rang. He said he's going to a gig in Birmingham.

2 "It's hopeless, isn't it?" she sighed. "All the socks are muddled up."

page 61

except – means 'to leave out'. Correct word: accept

arguement – argument

exsessive – excessive

disapear – disappear

sychologicle – psychological

affect – effect. 'Affect' is the verb, 'effect' the noun.

doesnt – doesn't. Always remember to include necessary apostrophes (see page 58).

ocasionaly – occasionally

choclate – chocolate

definately – definitely (stem word: finite)

vegatables – vegetables

losts – lots (presumably a careless error)

improof – improve

ourselfs – ourselves

page 65

Grade C

Bolton is not the worst place in the world, but it is not the best place either. It has a premiership football team and is close to motorways, so it is easy to travel around. However, if you are sixteen, you want more things to do and Bolton does not really have them.

I like to dance and mix with my friends. I also love ice skating. It is not possible to do either of these activities easily, though, because we are not provided with meeting areas like handily placed youth centres or ice rinks. It is hardly surprising we do so badly in the Winter Olympics. Many people agree with me and feel that the local council should apply themselves to giving us more of what we want.

A good youth centre, for example, would get teenagers off the streets and into doing something more worthwhile. As well as letting us let off some steam in the evening, the centres could organise trips out to other places nearby, so we could try different sports, play against other towns and cities and so on. They might even take us to the coast in the summer or to the countryside in the winter.

Having these opportunities would change many youngsters' attitudes. It might mean they would feel more positive about where they live and they might be more willing to contribute to charities and things like that. Instead of mugging little old men and stealing cars, they could sit in comfortable surroundings and drink coffee and tell their friends what is wrong with their lives. Parents would be happier too, knowing that their sons and daughters are safe.

So, I would say to all you readers that it is worthwhile to ask for more entertainments and centres to be provided. If we all put the council under pressure, I think they will change their policies and make Bolton an even better place to live. I am already proud of my town. If we all work together, we can make it even better.

page 69

Grade C

In Britain, we are living in a society that has a lot of money and where nobody needs to starve. People are paid well and most people have a job. Not everyone is living in a perfect state, but most of us have a roof over our head. It is easy to forget that not everyone is as lucky.

In the Third World, many people live very poor lives. They have to work all day for not much money and they cannot afford decent food or houses. Charities like Oxfam and Action Aid help them to help themselves, but we need to support the charities if they are to do that. An organisation like Water Aid only needs a small amount of money from each of us each month and they can provide wells and clean water. Can you think of a better cause? You should help them if you can.

What is more, even in England and Wales, some people still need support. There are some old people all on their own. The Salvation Army can help them. And there are drug addicts on the streets, with nowhere to turn. If we raise money for the charities that help them, we are doing our bit for our own society too.

It does not take much to be some kind of hero. My friend Katie did some fund-raising by doing a sponsored skip. We all thought she was crazy, but she managed to raise £85, which she gave to the St Mungo's Appeal, and will have made some poor people very happy over Christmas. You can even do a sponsored run, or hold a bring and buy sale. Every little helps.

It is better still if you get involved by helping to run the charity or actually care for others or deliver food parcels or even man the telephones. Doing work like that is better than sitting at home watching *EastEnders* or some reality show with second rate celebrities on it. If you help, you will be a real star, not just someone who wants to be more famous.

page 73

Grade C

Dear Miss Knowles,

Now that we have got the extra money from the government, I am writing on behalf of Year 11 to tell you what we think you should do with it. £100,000 is a lot of money, and we think that if it is spent properly, there will be many benefits for the whole school.

We would like you to consider spending it in different areas – to improve the sports facilities, the computer room and the library. However, we also think the students would like some rest and recreation areas. We have some classrooms that are not often used. We would like to see those developed so we can use them as common rooms at break and lunchtime.

The sports hall needs new equipment for gymnastics, volleyball and so on. If a chunk of the money is spent on improving it, the standard of fitness in the school might improve, which would be a good result. If more of the cash is spent on the dry play area and the fields, goalposts and cricket nets, then there is no doubt the school's sports results would improve too. That would help the school's reputation.

The computer room needs more printers and new mice, because students keep pinching the balls. Also, the library needs re-stocking and should have magazines each week, because that would encourage more students to go in there. Hey presto, our exam results would then start improving too.

Then, if we had common rooms as well, we would be out of the rain and better able to concentrate in lessons and we would not be hanging around outside in the cold. It would not cost much to provide drinks machines – which might even pay for themselves – and some games, like pool and darts boards. The students would then be much more positive about school and behaviour would improve.

So you see, if you spend the money in these ways, the school will be a much better place. We hope you take our ideas seriously.

Yours sincerely …

page 77

Grade C

I love playing badminton. Once I have finished my homework each evening, I go straight down to my local sports hall. I am allowed to play badminton for as long as I want, provided no one else is waiting for a court. This is because I am a member of the Arnside Racquets Squash and Badminton Association.

I started to play when I was just six years old. My mum says I could always hit the shuttle but it did not usually go where I wanted it to. By the age of twelve, I was playing for the junior team and now I represent the seniors. I sometimes play singles when we have matches, and I am always in the doubles team.

We play matches all year round, because in our area there is no real 'season' for our sport. This means that once a month, on average, I play a home match and once a month I play away. That is always even more fun, because all the players in the team get on really well, and we have a laugh together. Once they even threw me in a swimming pool when we won our last

match and avoided relegation. I think it was because I had done well, not because no one likes me.

I have won quite a lot of trophies. I was second in the county two years ago, in my age group, and have played in the national championships. Unfortunately I was knocked out early on. I had a cold and did not do well. Anyway, in my bedroom there are twelve shields and some certificates framed on the wall. That is not to be big-headed, just because they inspire me to try even harder in the future.

Since I am so involved in badminton, I have little time to do anything else. My dad always says that isn't a problem, so long as I am enjoying what I do. My ambition is to play for England, and for Great Britain in the Olympics, and he approves of that, so I'll just keep on practising. I think that he is hoping I'll be able to get him lots of free tickets for the finals – but I just want to wear the team's track suit and win a gold medal.

page 81

Grade C

Everything that goes wrong for me seems to be connected to my friends. If there is a problem at school or at home, I have to sort it out by getting my friends sorted out first. That is just the way it goes.

Take getting to school on time. I always get up early, but then my mates come round to the house late, so we get to school late. I get into trouble from my parents if the school gives me detention, so I have to try to talk to my friends and make them understand what is happening. I even end up going to school on my own sometimes, when they look like letting me down. On occasions, I might have to grab a lift from Marcie who lives next door, and I don't like her parents at all. That's how serious it is.

My friends also used to get me into trouble when we were out at nights. Once or twice, the police were involved. It came about because we were hanging around the old people's bungalows, and they hated it because they thought we were going to break in and steal all their Abba CDs or throw bricks through their windows. Anyway, my parents made my life a misery again and grounded me for about a million years, so I told my friends we had to find a new place. Now, we usually have a laugh just down the road from the police station, which is quite ironic, really.

The worst problem I have ever had, though, was when I got a really nice girlfriend called Suki, and she said I had to choose between my mates and her. She didn't like them. She said they were a bad influence. One night she just said, "All right, what's it going to be?"

I've never liked being told what to do, so I said I was just going to do what I felt like. That sorted out the problem straight away, because she left and I haven't been out with her again.

Overall, I believe I can deal with problems with my friends and can usually sort things out without making situations worse. Now, my friends are becoming more sensible all the time, so there are less likely to be problems in the future.

Grade C

Most of my life out of school is spent in the local park. That might not sound very interesting, but the park is where all my friends meet, and it has different parts, because it is so big. We can play around in the adventure playground, with its skateboard section; we can play football on any of the fields, or in the arena. We can have a laugh at people on the pitch-and-putt course; or we can just frighten the ducks down by the lake.

Sometimes, when we are on the rides and swings, we must look like young children again, but we don't care. There's a slide that's about ten metres high, there's a roundabout that turns us into a blur, and a brilliant rocker that takes eight of us. We throw it forwards and back and you can hear the girls screaming at the other side of the park.

We go on the pitches too, but they are always full of mud which oozes over your trainers and makes the knees of your jeans stick to your legs. Of course, at weekends the nets are up and teams pour into the park to play league matches. There are blues and reds and whites everywhere, and people chanting.

At weekends, too, we hang around the pitch-and-putt course, because it's even funnier than the bowling greens. Many of the old men playing bowls are actually quite good, even if they do all wear flat caps, but the pitch-and-putters mostly haven't any idea at all. On sunny days, there are kids running around pushing golf balls ahead of them (thirty hits to get to the green), women swinging and missing and men smashing the bushes about trying to find their missing ball. It's brilliant.

I know that the park seems like a strange place to spend all your time, but it's better than just watching television and it's not all the same. In fact, when the fair comes in summer and it's full of frying onions and rides, it's one of the best places in the world.

Index

adjectives 14, 56, 57, 76
adverbs 56
advice writing 70–3
  ideas, organising 70
  problems, outlining 70
  solutions, offering 70, 72
  techniques 73
  tone 71, 73
  vocabulary 14
alliteration 38, 41
anecdotes
  argumentative writing 12, 13, 65
  persuasive writing 68, 69
apostrophes 58
arguments/argumentative writing
  10–13, 62–5
  conclusions 10, 11, 64
  developing an argument 64
  following an argument 10–13
  language 12
  point of view 10, 62, 63, 65
  structure 10–11, 63
  techniques 12–13, 65
associations, words and 40
assonance 39
audience
  advice writing 71
  argumentative writing 12
  media and non-fiction 8, 12, 14,
    27
  persuasive writing 66
  in writing tasks 50, 54, 86
autobiographies 23

Blessing 39, 40
block capitals 19, 27
bold text 18, 19
brackets 59

captions 18
colloquial language/slang 14, 16
colons 59
columns 18
commands 14, 22, 40, 55, 71
commas 40, 58, 87
connectives 53, 58, 63, 65
content
  poetry 32
  writing tasks 50
contrasts 12, 13, 16, 68, 81, 84
cultures and traditions 30–1

dashes 59
descriptive writing 82–5, 87
  conclusions 84, 85
  describing what you know 82
  detail 55, 83, 84

introduction 83
structure 82
techniques 84–5

emotive language 16, 17, 56, 67,
  69
emphasis 40, 41
exaggeration
  argumentative writing 12, 13
  media and non-fiction writing 16,
    17
  persuasive writing 68
examples, giving
  advice writing 72, 73
  argumentative writing 12, 13
  information writing 76
  media and non-fiction writing 8,
    16
  persuasive writing 68, 69
  poetry 30, 39, 41
exclamation marks 15, 58
exclamations 55
explanation writing 78–81
  introduction 79
  language 80
  structure and planning 78–9
  techniques 81
  vocabulary 14

facts
  comparing texts 9
  information writing 75
  media and non-fiction writing 8,
    9
fonts 18
from Search For My Tongue 30, 38
from Unrelated Incidents 30, 33

Half-Caste 30, 36, 38
headings 18, 22
headlines 18, 19, 21
humour
  argumentative writing 12, 13
  descriptive writing 85, 87
  media and non-fiction writing 16
  persuasive writing 68
Hurricane Hits England 30, 39

ideas
  developing 51, 53
  linking 53
  organising 70, 74
  presentation 71
  structuring 51, 66
  thinking of 50
imagery 15, 57, 68, 81
  see also metaphors; similes

information writing 74–7
  clear information 75
  facts and opinions 75
  ideas, organising 74
  information, choosing 74
  personal response 75, 76
  techniques 77
inverted commas 20, 26, 27, 59, 87
Island Man 31, 33, 38, 40, 42, 44, 45
italic text 18

language
  argumentative writing 12
  explanation writing 80
  media and non-fiction writing 12,
    14–17, 21
  persuasive writing 67
  poetry 30, 32, 33, 34, 35, 38–41,
    46
layout and presentational devices
  media and non-fiction writing
    18–19, 21
  poetry 37
Limbo 31, 36, 37, 39
lists
  argumentative writing 12, 13, 65
  media and non-fiction writing 16,
    17
  poetry 40
  in writing tasks 53, 58
logos 18, 22
Love After Love 40, 41

media and non-fiction writing 6–27
  argumentative writing 10–13
  exam paper 6–7
  facts and opinions 8–9
  language 12–13, 14–17, 21
  layout and presentational devices
    18–19, 21
  text comparison 6, 24–5
  text type analysis 21–3
metaphors 15, 17, 38, 41, 57
mnemonics 61

Night of the Scorpion 31, 36, 37, 38
non-fiction *see* media and non-fiction
  writing
Not My Business 30, 33, 34, 35, 36
Nothing's Changed 31, 33, 38, 44

onomatopoeia 39
opinions
  comparing texts 9
  information writing 75
  media and non-fiction writing 8,
    9, 26

paragraphs
  advice writing 72
  argumentative writing 10, 63, 64
  concluding paragraphs 10, 11, 21, 45, 52, 64, 72
  descriptive writing 84
  information writing 75, 77
  introductory paragraphs 10, 18, 19, 21, 44, 52, 53, 63, 75
  linking 52, 53, 75, 77, 84
  media and non-fiction writing 18, 19, 21
  paragraph length 14, 21, 53
  writing tasks 52–3, 86
pattern in poetry 36
persuasive writing 14, 66–9, 73
  language 67
  structuring ideas 66
  techniques 68–9
  vocabulary 14
photographs and graphics 18, 19, 21, 22
planning
  advice writing 70
  argumentative writing 64
  descriptive writing 82
  explanation writing 78–9
  information writing 74
  persuasive writing 66
  poetry questions 42
  in writing tasks 50–1, 86
plurals, forming 60
poetry 28–47
  attitude 34–5, 46
  comparison 41, 42–5, 46, 47
  content 32
  cultures and traditions 30–1, 33
  exam paper 28–9
  language 30, 32, 33, 34, 35, 38–41, 46
  message 33, 35
  people and settings 31
  poetic techniques 38–9, 46
  quotations 43, 46
  situations and problems 31
  structure 36–7
point of view
  argumentative writing 10, 62, 63, 65
  persuasive writing 69
prefixes 60
Presents from my Aunts in Pakistan 30, 40, 41, 47
pull-quotes 19
punctuation
  descriptive writing 87
  media and non-fiction writing 15
  poetry 40
  in writing tasks 58–9

purpose of the text
  advice writing 71
  media and non-fiction writing 8, 10, 12, 14
  poetry 39, 41
  in writing tasks 50, 54, 86, 87

question marks 15, 58
quotations
  argumentative writing 12, 65
  descriptive writing 87
  media and non-fiction writing 16, 18, 19, 20, 21, 25, 26
  poetry 43, 46
  pull-quotes 19

raising your grade
  media and non-fiction writing 7, 26–7
  poetry questions 46–7
  writing tasks 86–7
reading skills 4, 5, 7, 29
refrain in poetry 36
repetition
  argumentative writing 12
  persuasive writing 68
  poetry 36, 38, 39, 40
  writing tasks 56
rhetoric 68
rhetorical questions
  argumentative writing 12, 13, 65
  media and non-fiction writing 16, 17
  persuasive writing 68, 69
  in writing tasks 55
rhyme in poetry 38
rhythm in poetry 38

sarcasm 81
semi-colons 59
senses in descriptive writing 83
sentences
  construction 14
  length 14, 16, 23, 40, 41, 53, 54–5, 65, 69, 86
  media and non-fiction writing 16, 23
  persuasive writing 69
  in poetry 40, 41
  single word sentences 54
  topic sentences 53, 63, 65
  in writing tasks 53, 54–5, 86
similes 15, 17, 34, 38, 41, 57, 85
slang *see* colloquial language
slogans 18
speech marks *see* inverted commas
spell checker programs 61

spelling 60–1, 87
  checking and correcting 61
  common misspellings 61
  plurals 60
  prefixes and suffixes 60
  strategies 61
  verbs 60
spider diagrams 51, 74
stanzas in poetry 36
straplines 18, 21
style 16–17, 50, 54
  formal 16
  informal 16
  stylistic techniques 16
subheadings 18, 71
subordinate clauses 54
suffixes 60
symbolism 38, 39, 47

text bubbles 79
text comparison
  media and non-fiction writing 6, 9, 24–5
  poetry 42–5
text types 21–3
textual references 20
This Room 31, 38, 40, 41, 47
tone 32, 50, 54, 71, 73
topic sentences 53, 63, 65
Two Scavengers in a Truck, Two Beautiful People in a Mercedes 31, 36, 37

verbs, forming 60
vocabulary
  advice writing 14
  argumentative writing 14
  explanation writing 14
  interesting and unusual words 14, 56, 86
  persuasive writing 14
  in writing tasks 56–7
Vultures 31, 32, 33, 34, 36, 40

web pages 22
What Were They Like? 30, 31
writing skills 4, 5, 49
writing tasks 48–61
  exam paper 48–9
  types of writing 62–87